Praise for *I Think I Am In Friend-Love With You*

❝ Look around. You won't find anything sweeter than this lonely little book anywhere in your immediate vicinity. Unless for some reason there's, like, a bunny knitting a scarf for a puppy. That might be sweeter. Aside from that, this book is definitely your best bet. ❞

—AVERY MONSEN, coauthor of *K Is for Knifeball* and *All My Friends Are Dead*

❝ This is one of my favorite comics ever, a sweet ode to platonic love that will echo through the ages. ❞

—MARI NAOMI, author of *Kiss & Tell*

❝ Funny and beautifully drawn, *I Think I Am In Friend-Love With You* is the bittersweet tale of friendships in the age of social media in which many can relate. ❞

—ESTHER PEARL WATSON, author of *Unlovable*

❝ The warmth of Yumi's soft brushstrokes and vulnerability of her words make me feel less alone in this weird world. I think I am in book-love. ❞

—LISA HANAWALT, author of *My Dirty Dumb Eyes*

Published by
Adams Media, a division of F+W Media, Inc.
57 Littlefield Street, Avon, MA 02322. U.S.A.
www.adamsmedia.com

ISBN 10: 1-4405-7302-6
ISBN 13: 978-1-4405-7302-6
eISBN 10: 1-4405-7303-4
eISBN 13: 978-1-4405-7303-3

Printed in the United States of America.

10 9 8 7

Many of the designations used by manufacturers and sellers to distinguish their product are claimed as trademarks. Where those designations appear in this book and F+W Media was aware of a trademark claim, the designations have been printed with initial capital letters.

This book is available at quantity discounts for bulk purchases.
For information, please call 1-800-289-0963.

I HAVE A CONFESSION TO MAKE.

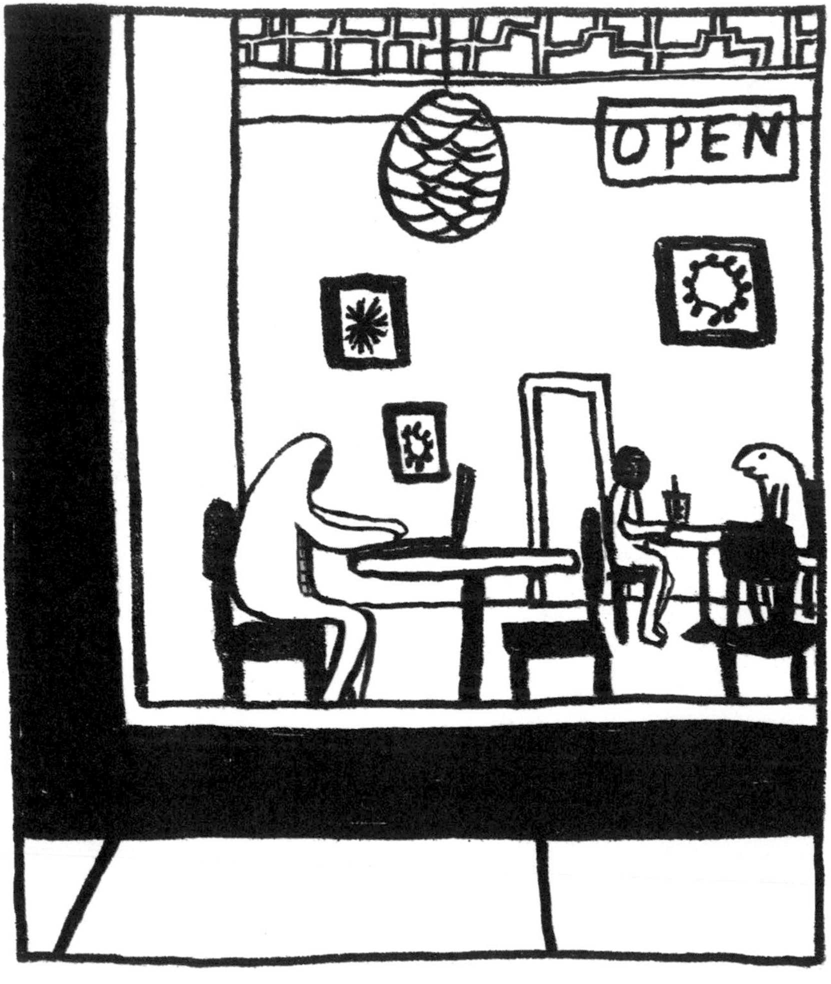
OPEN

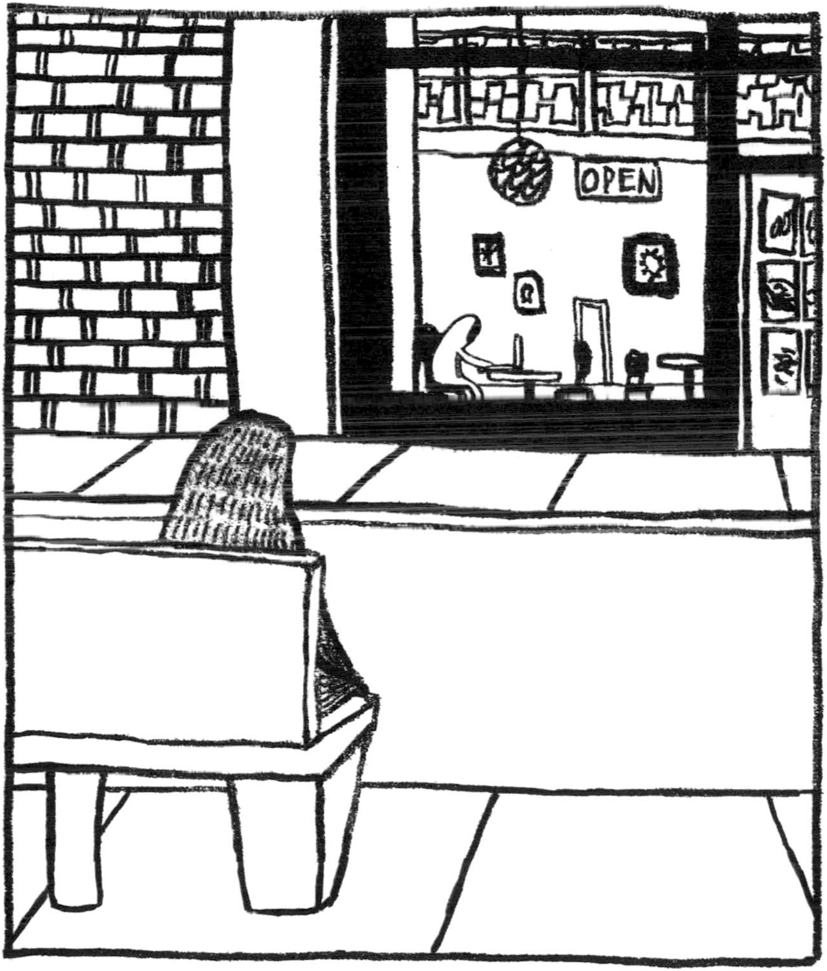
OPEN

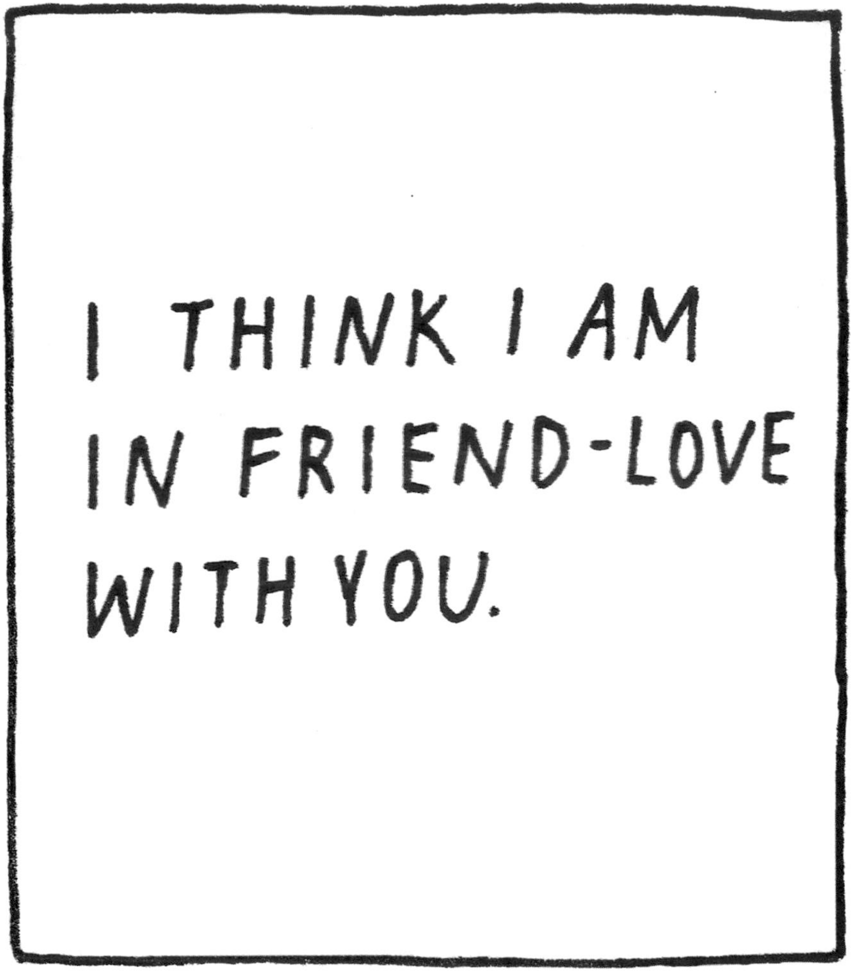
I THINK I AM
IN FRIEND-LOVE
WITH YOU.

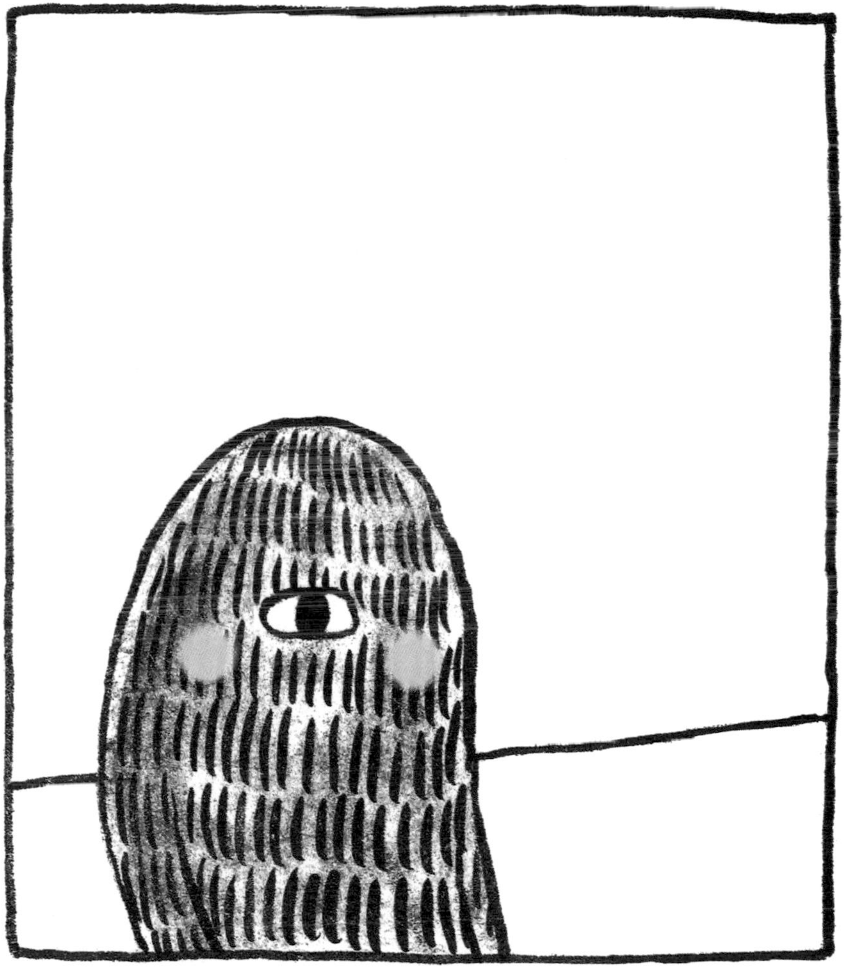

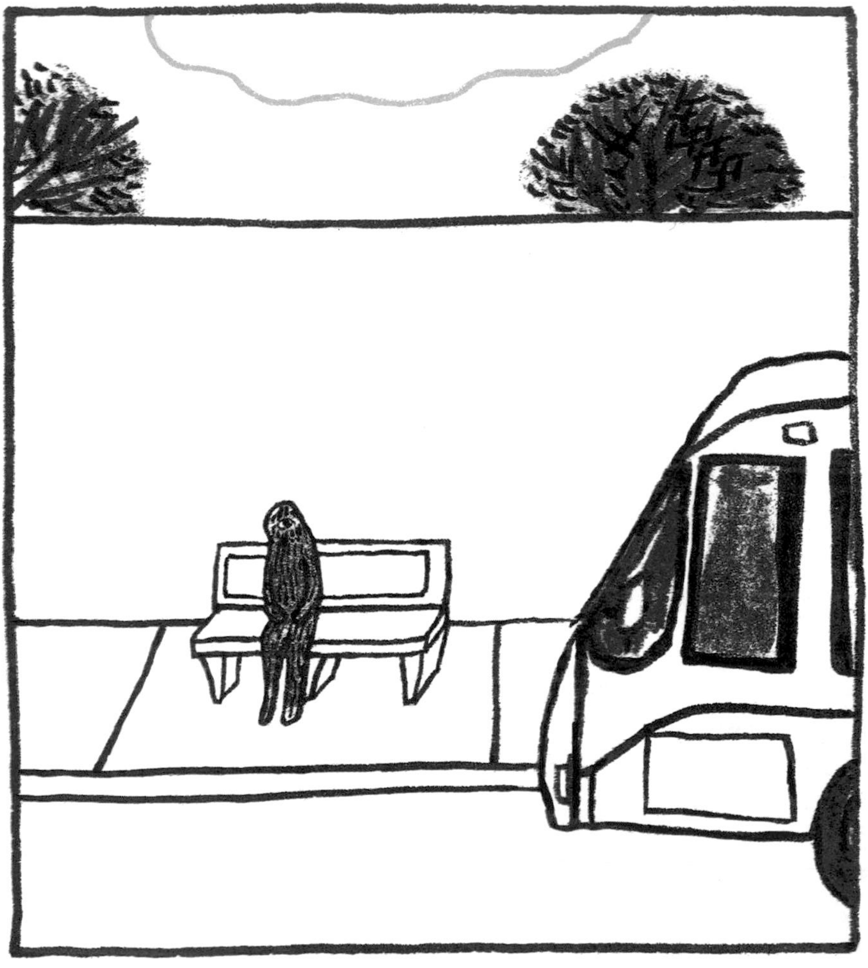

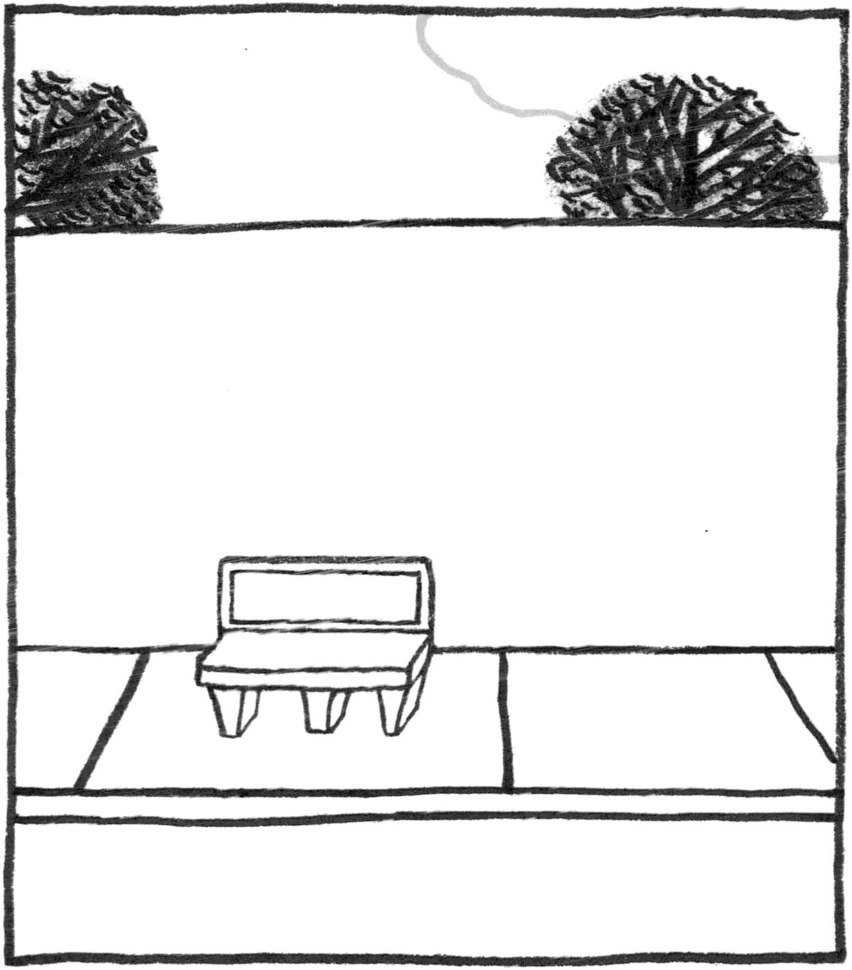

I DON'T WANT
TO DATE YOU
OR EVEN MAKE
OUT WITH YOU.

BECAUSE THAT
WOULD BE WEIRD.

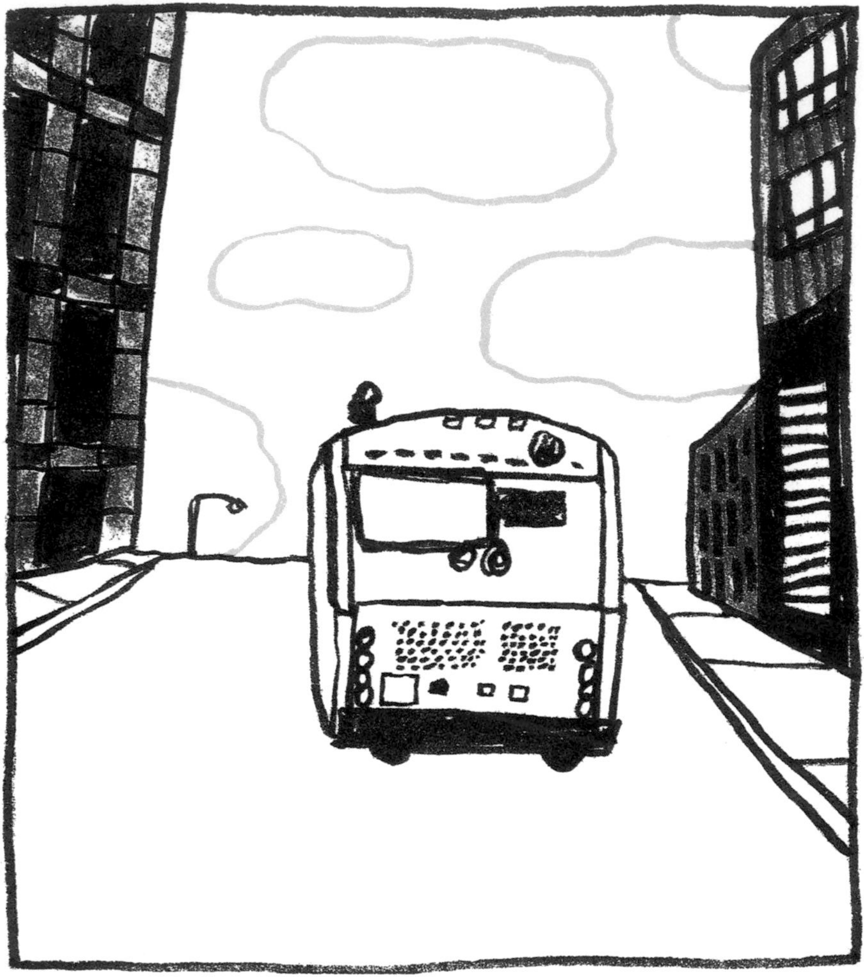

I JUST SO
DESPERATELY
WANT FOR YOU
TO THINK

THAT I AM THIS SUPER-AWESOME PERSON

BECAUSE I THINK
YOU ARE A
SUPER-AWESOME
PERSON

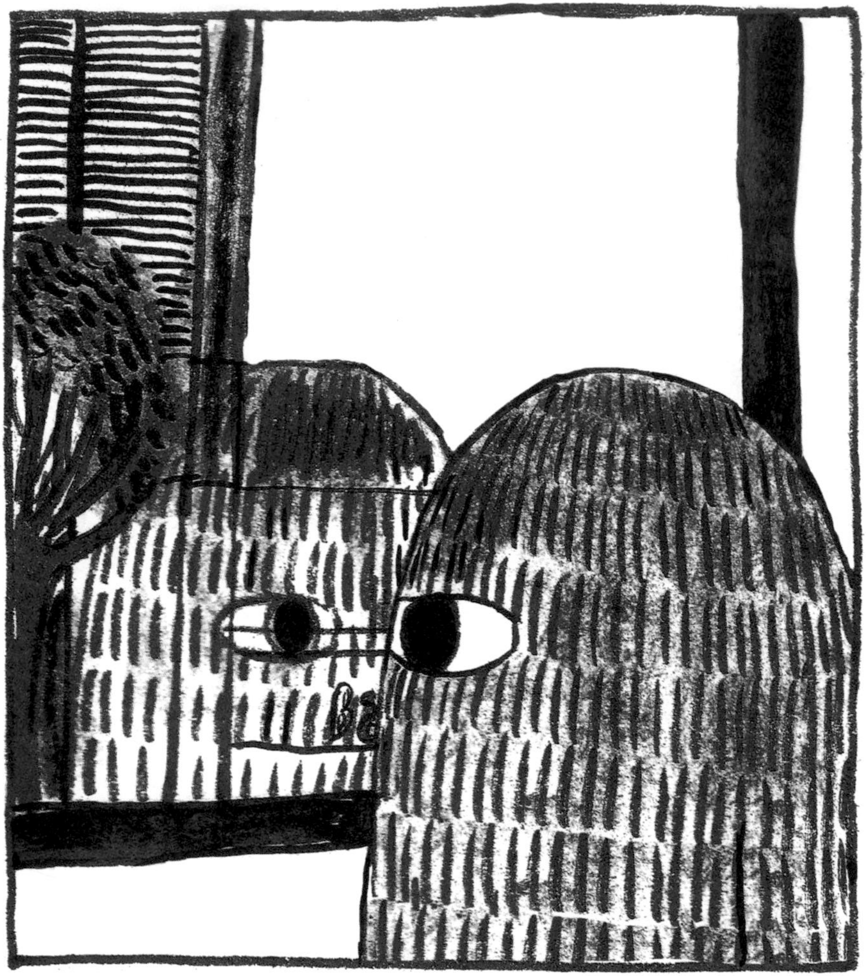

AND I WANT TO SPEND A LOT OF TIME HANGING OUT WITH YOU.

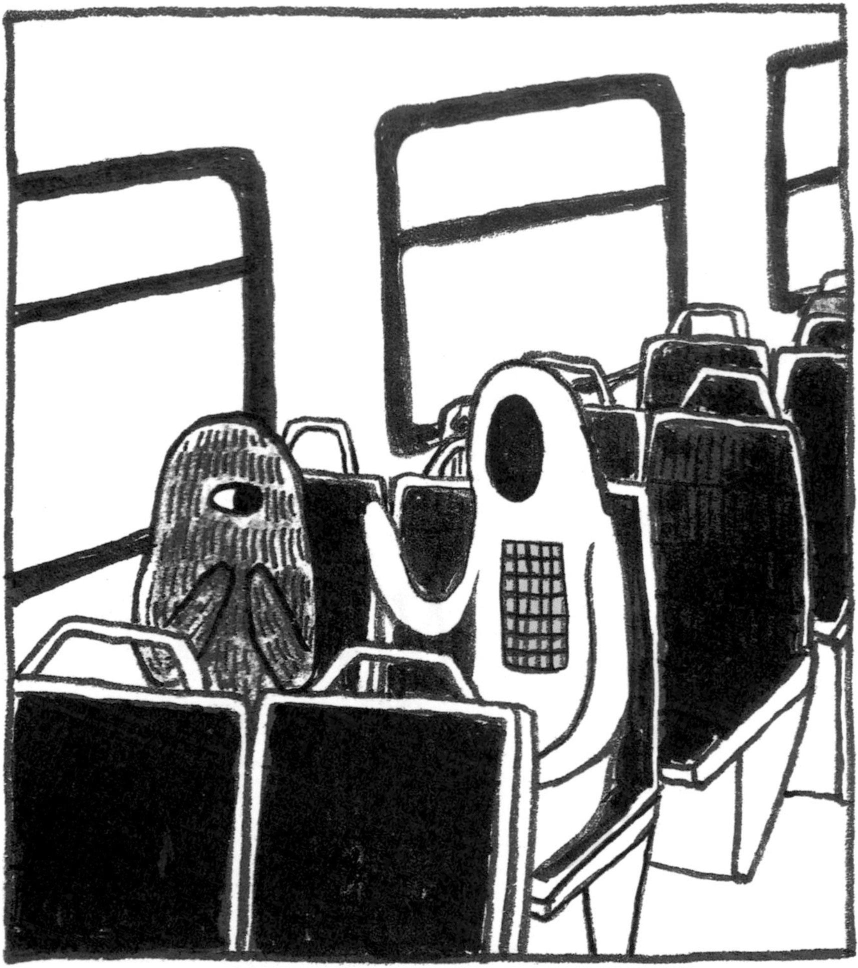

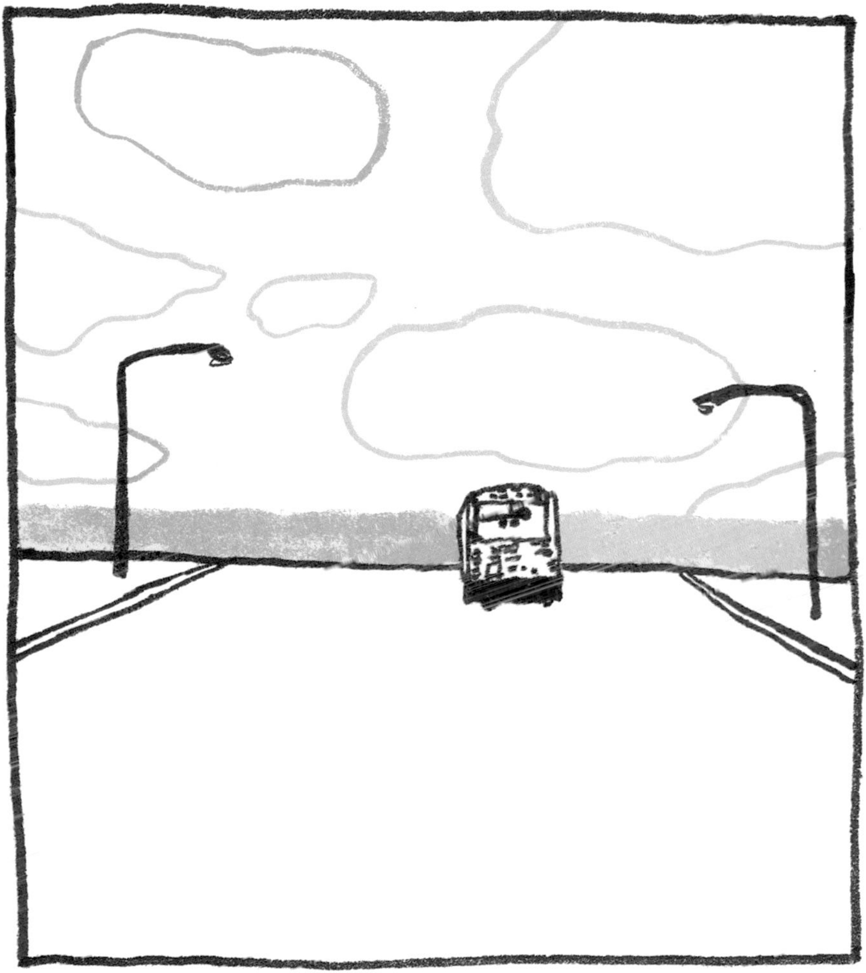

I WANT TO
FACEBOOK-CHAT
WITH YOU AFTER
MIDNIGHT.

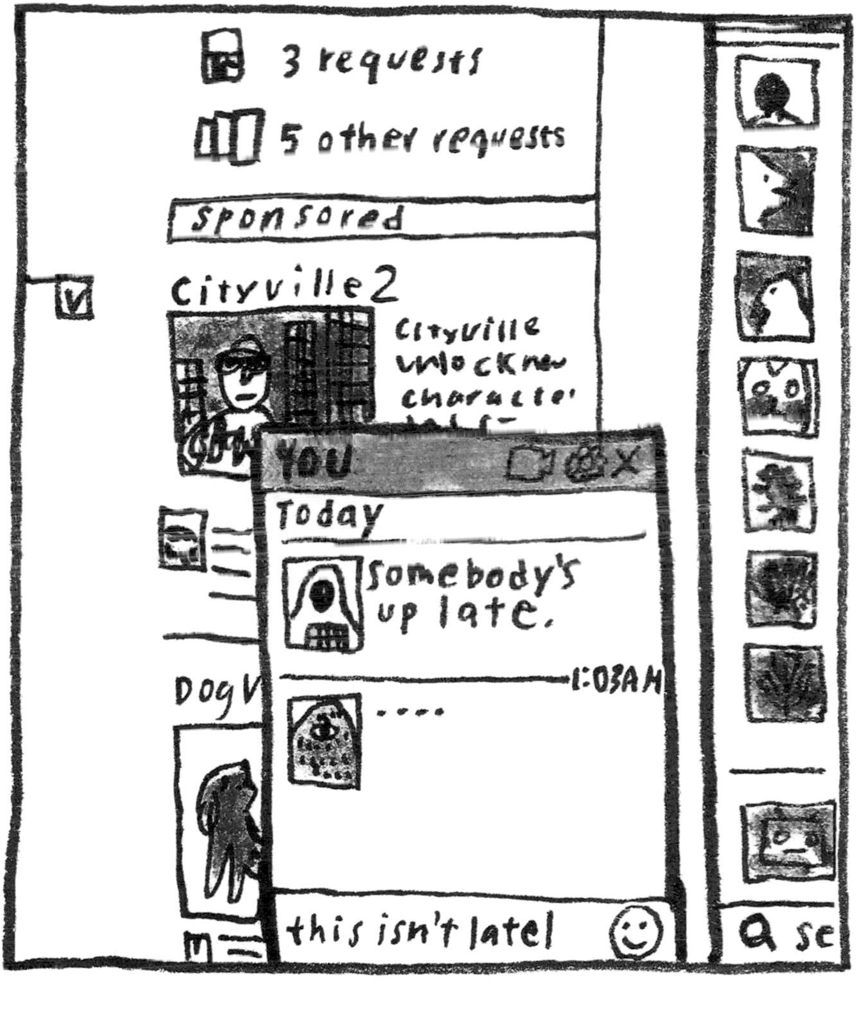
3 requests
5 other requests
Sponsored
Cityville2
Cityville unlock new character
DogV
YOU
Today
Somebody's up late.
1:03AM
....
this isn't late!

I WANT YOU TO TEXT ME TO HANG OUT.

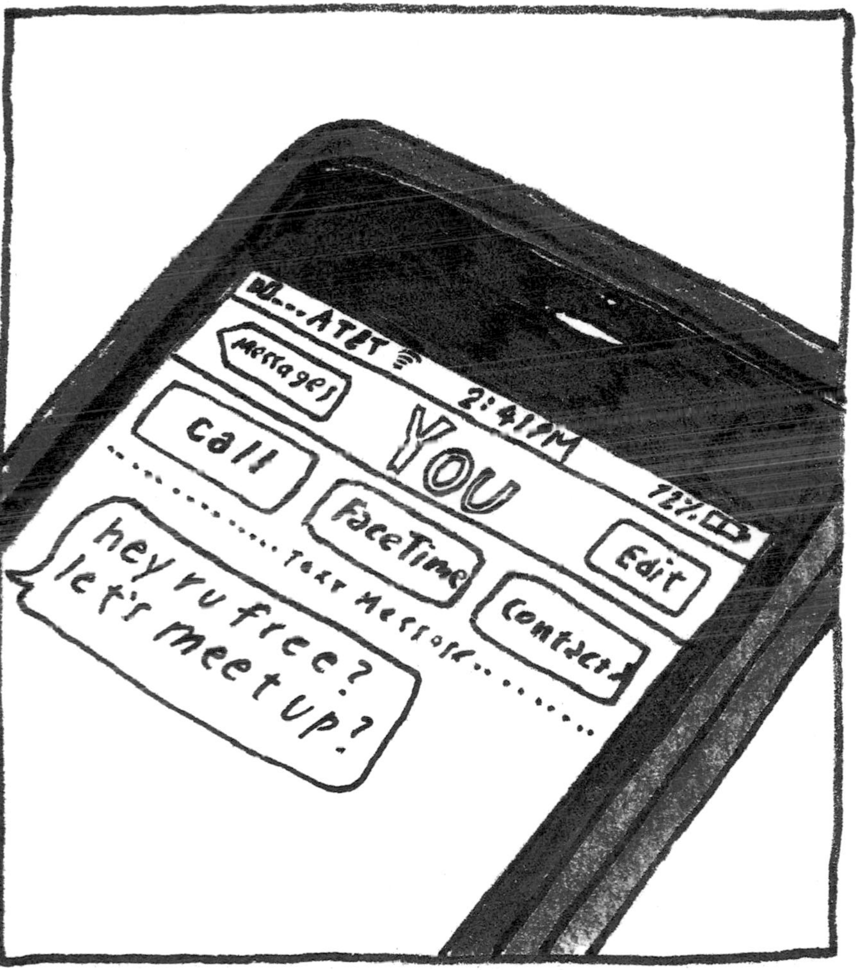
AT&T
Messages
2:41PM
YOU
72%
call
FaceTime
Edit
Contacts
Text Message
hey ru free?
let's meet up?

IN A PLATONIC
WAY, OF COURSE.

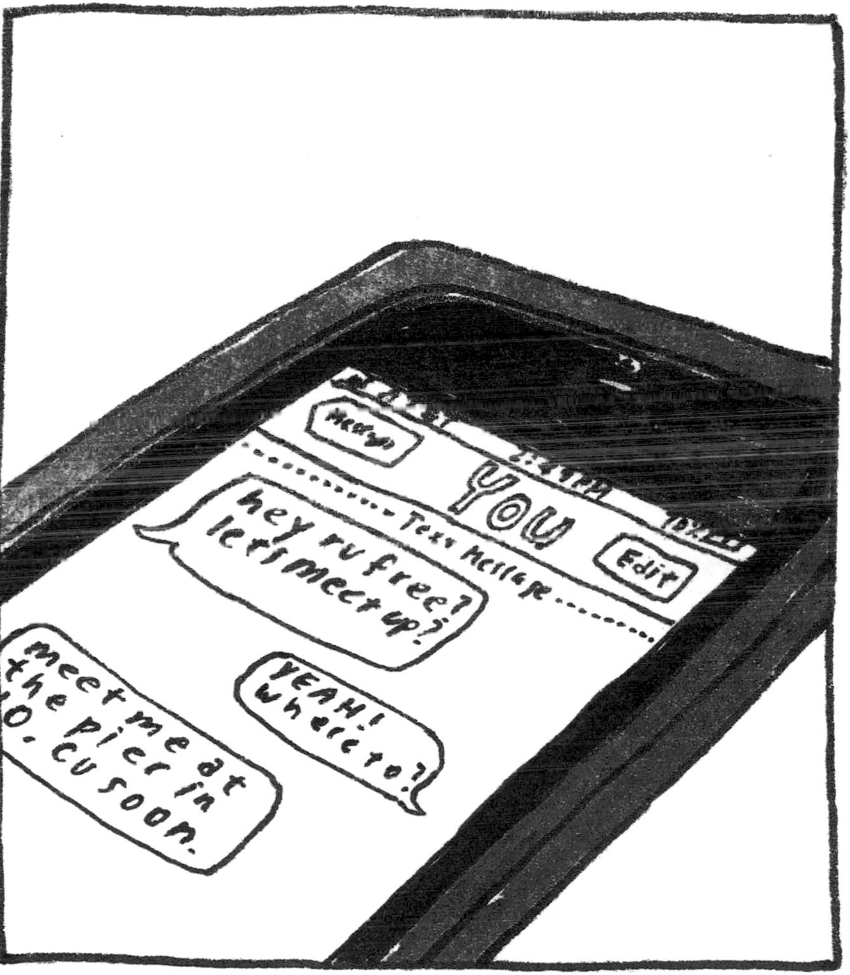
YOU
Edit
Text Message
hey ru free? lets meet up?
YEAH! where to?
meet me at the pier in 0. CU soon.

I WANT US TO
@ REPLY TO EACH
OTHER'S TWEETS

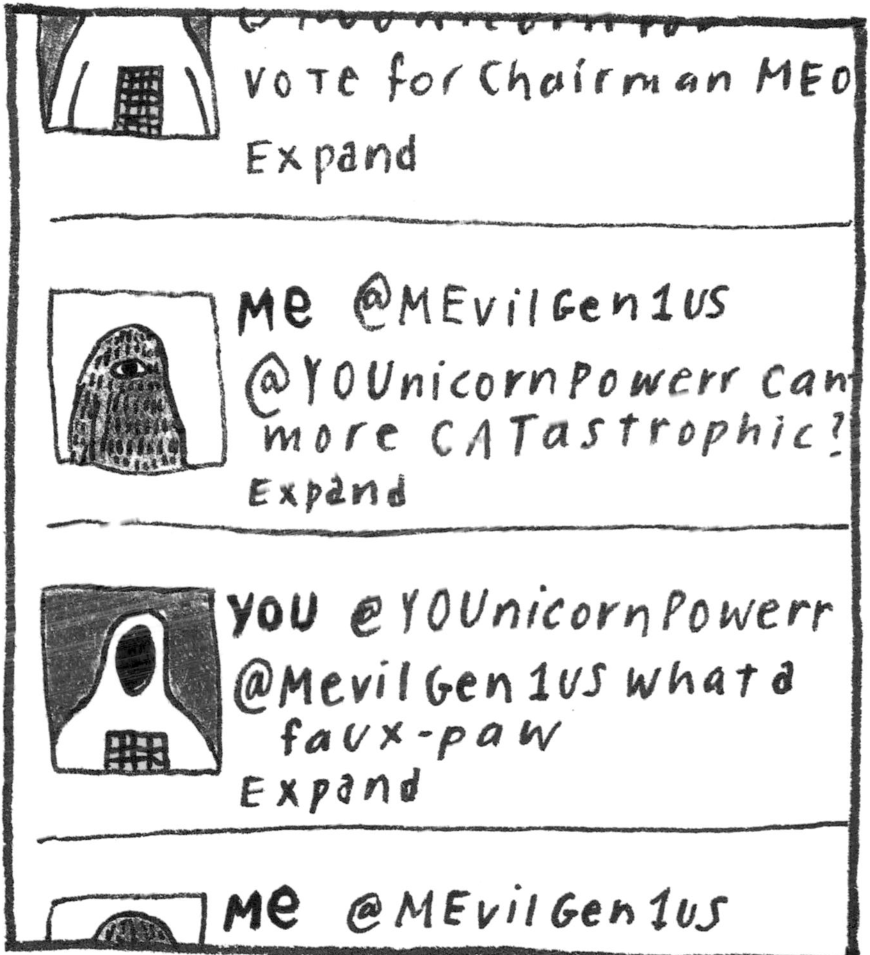

vote for Chairman MEO
Expand
ME @MEvilGen1US
@YOUnicornPowerr Can
more CATastrophic?
Expand
YOU @YOUnicornPowerr
@MevilGen1US what a
faux-paw
Expand
ME @MEvilGen1US

AND REBLOG
EACH OTHER'S
TUMBLR REBLOGS

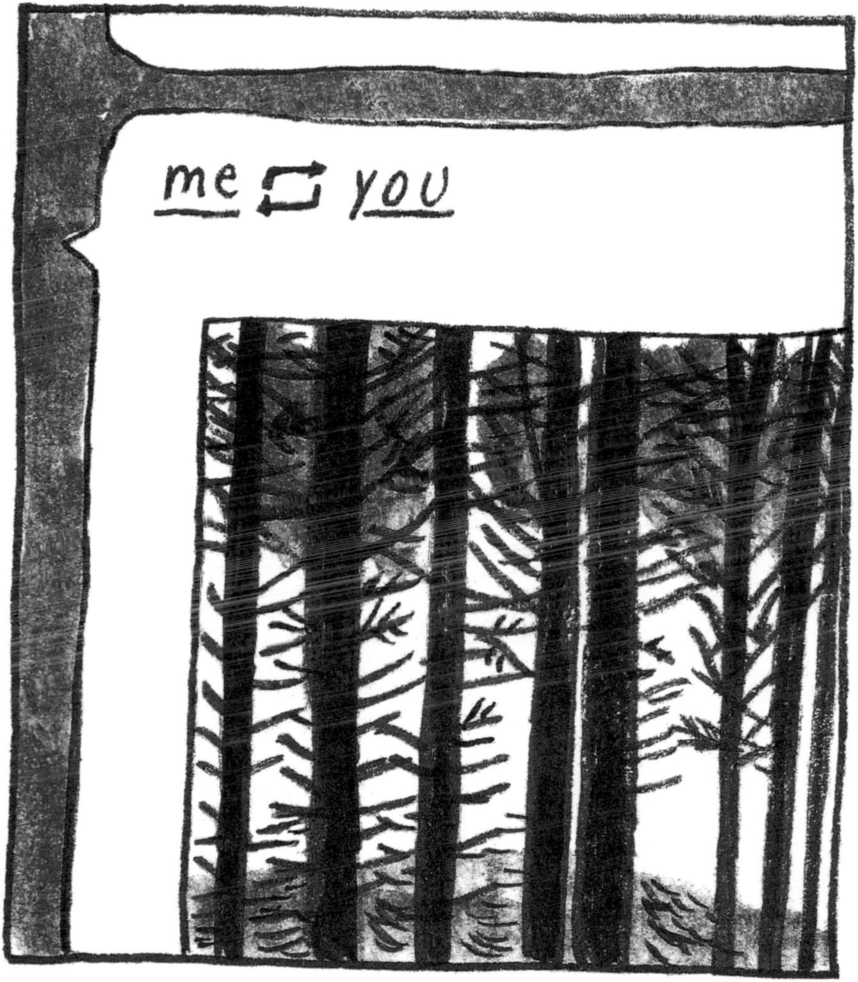
me ⇄ you

BECAUSE WHAT
YOU FIND TO BE
BEAUTIFUL,
FUNNY AND
HEARTBREAKING
IN THIS WORLD

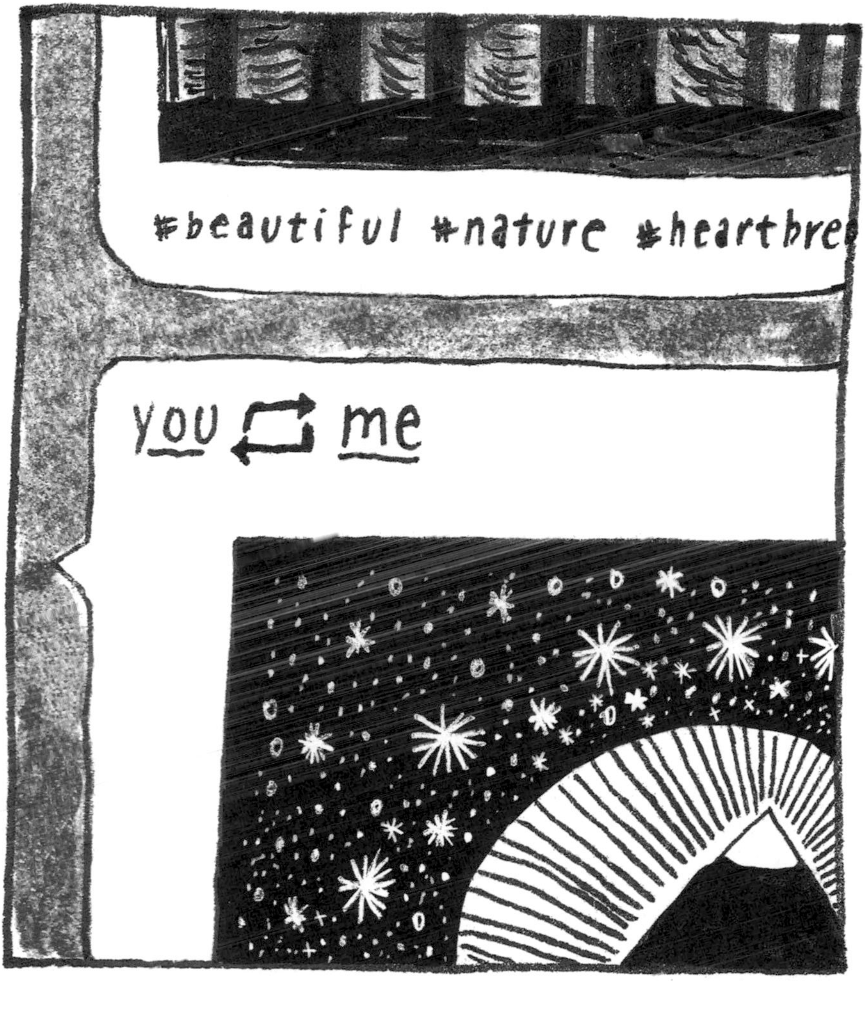
#beautiful #nature #heartbre
you me

IS WHAT I FIND
TO BE BEAUTIFUL,
FUNNY AND
HEARTBREAKING
IN THIS WORLD.

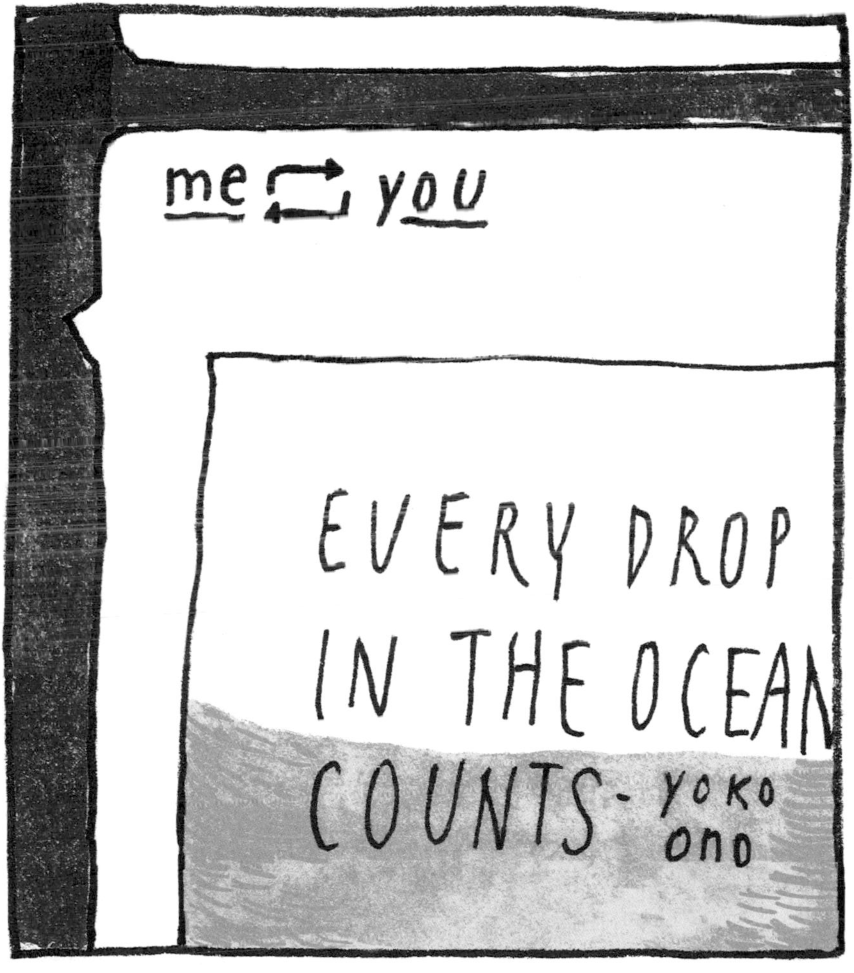
me ⇄ you
EVERY DROP IN THE OCEAN COUNTS - yoko ono

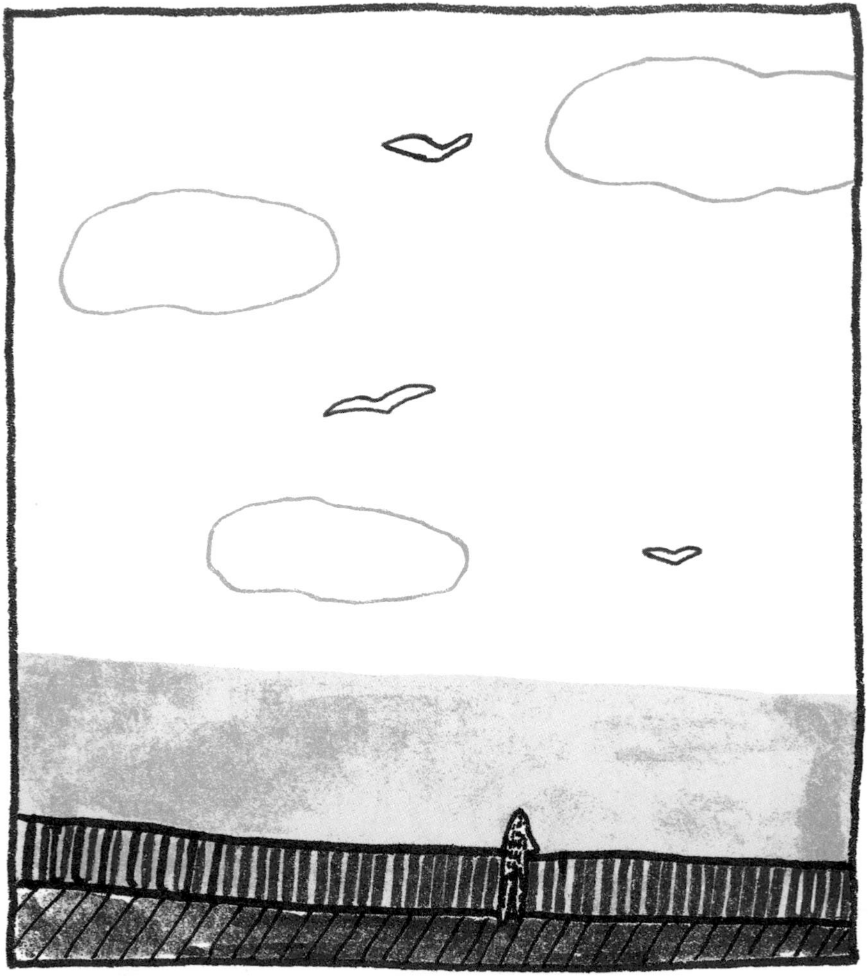

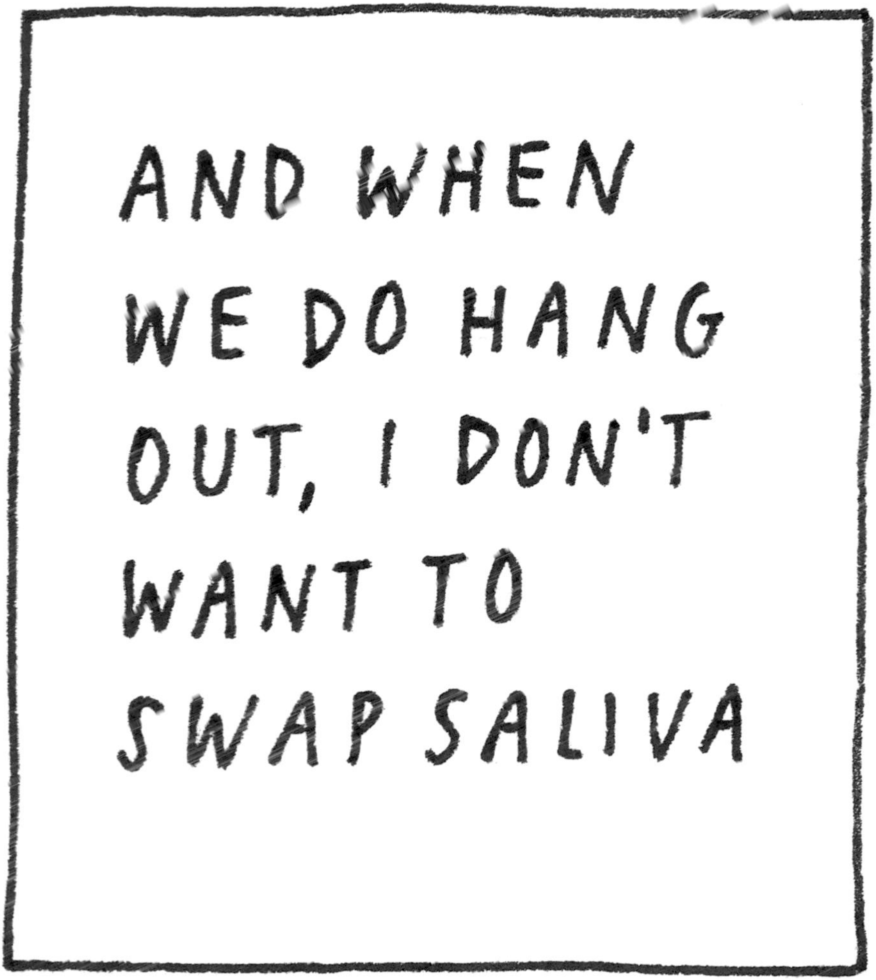
AND WHEN WE DO HANG OUT, I DON'T WANT TO SWAP SALIVA

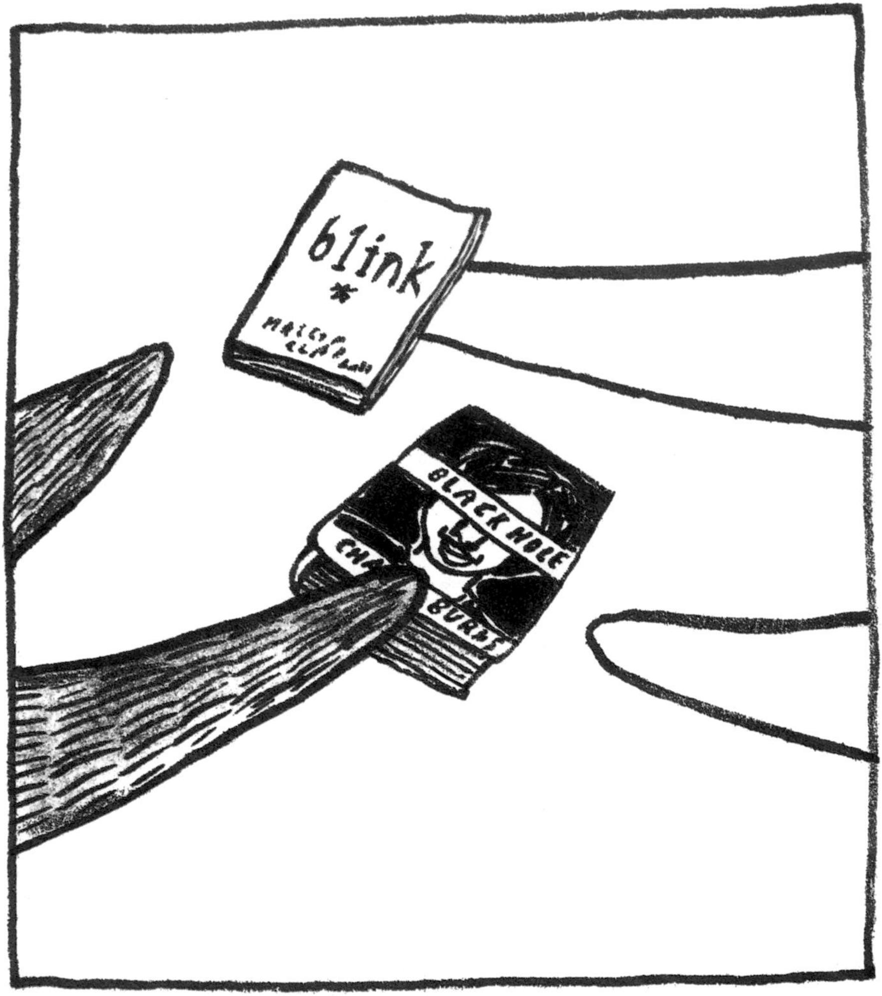
blink
BLACK HOLE
CHA
BURNS

I JUST WANT TO SWAP FAVORITE BOOKS.

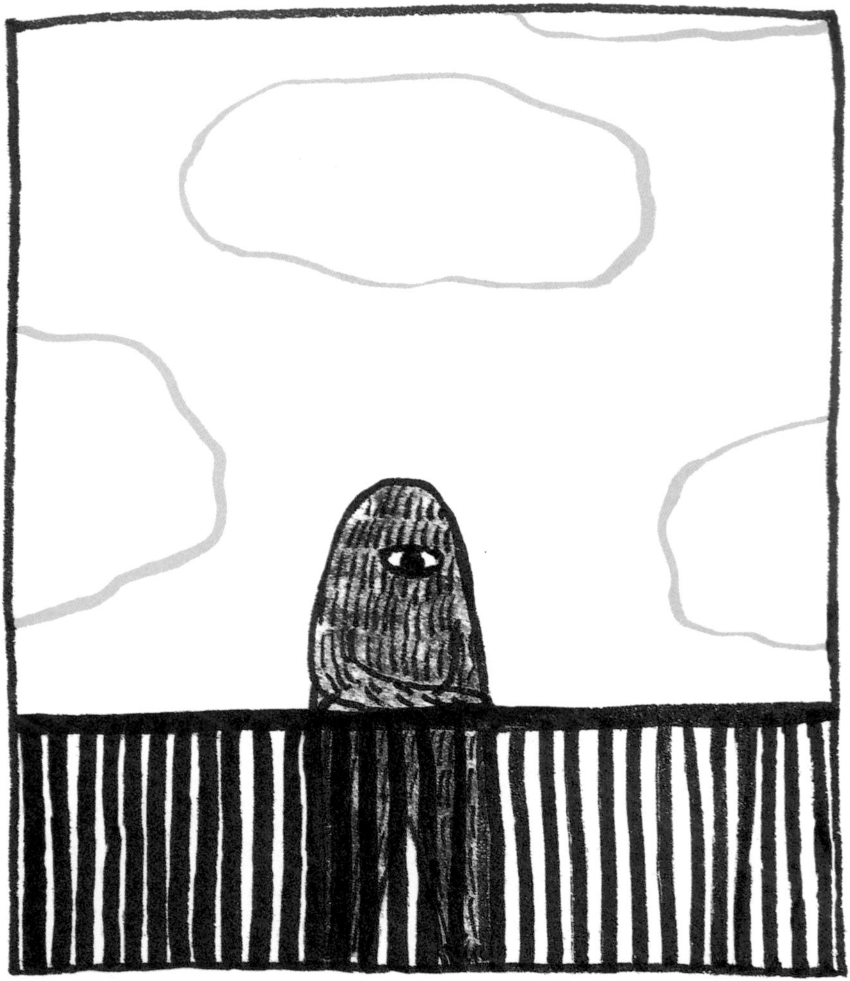

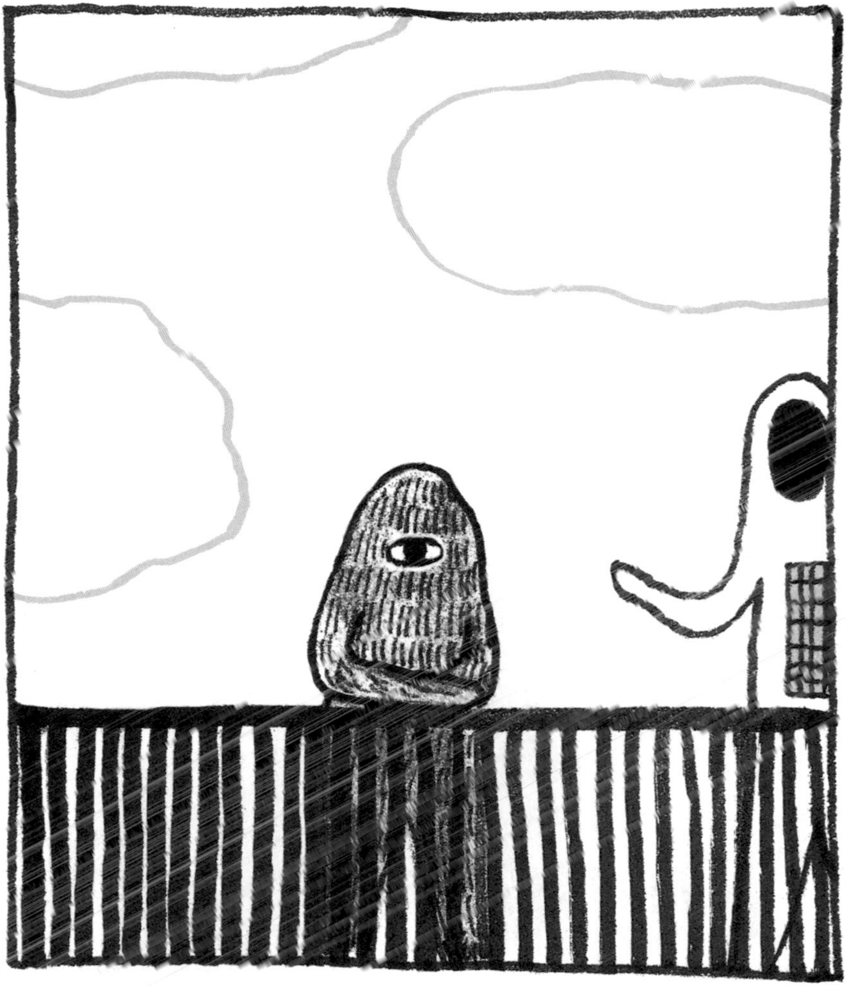

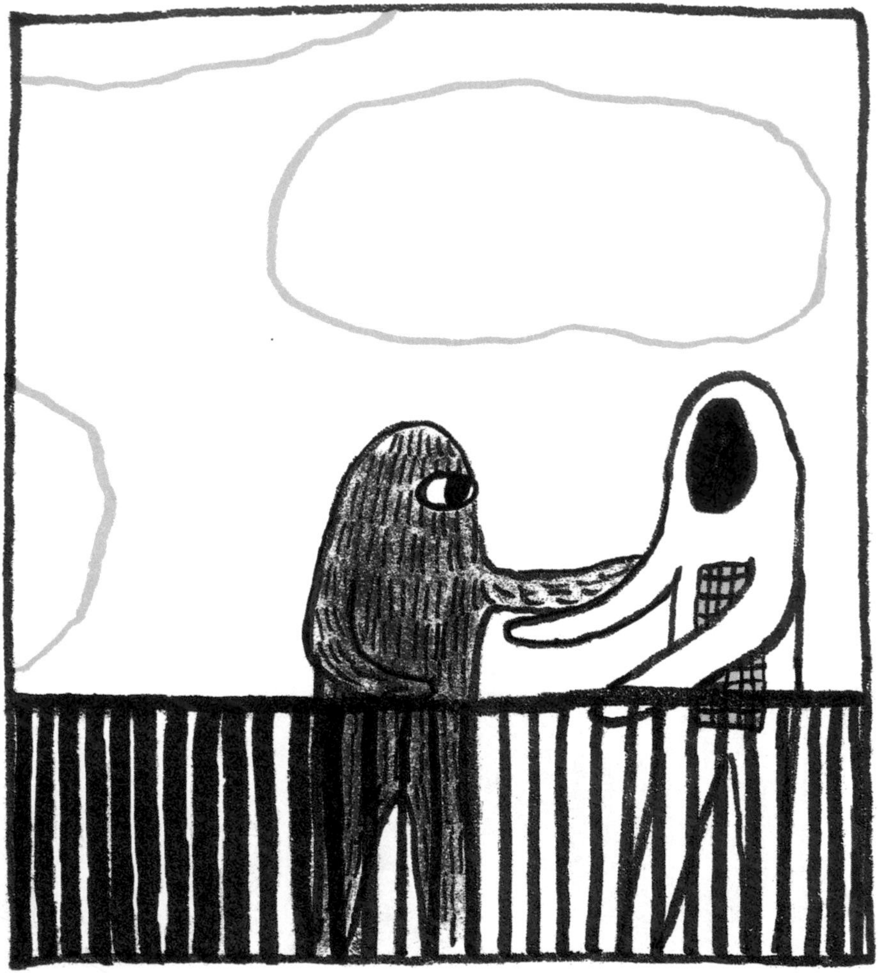

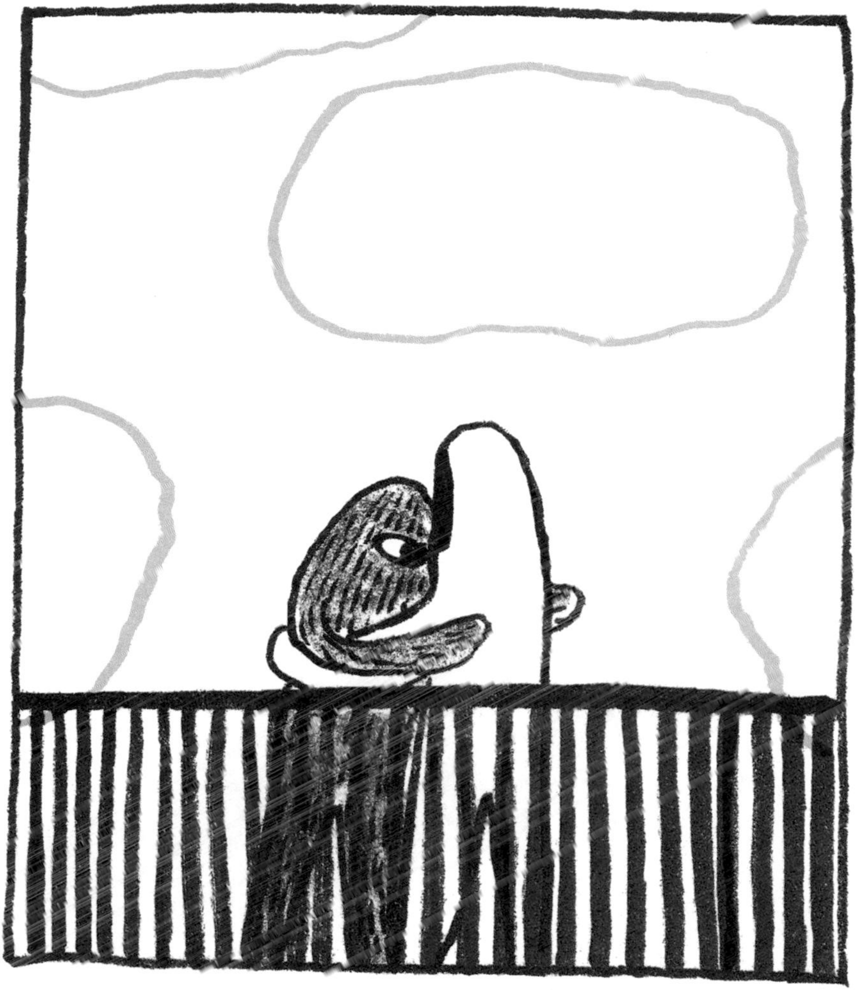

I WANT OUR HELLO/
GOOD-BYE HUGS
TO BE A FEW
BEATS LONGER
THAN A CASUAL
FRIEND HUG

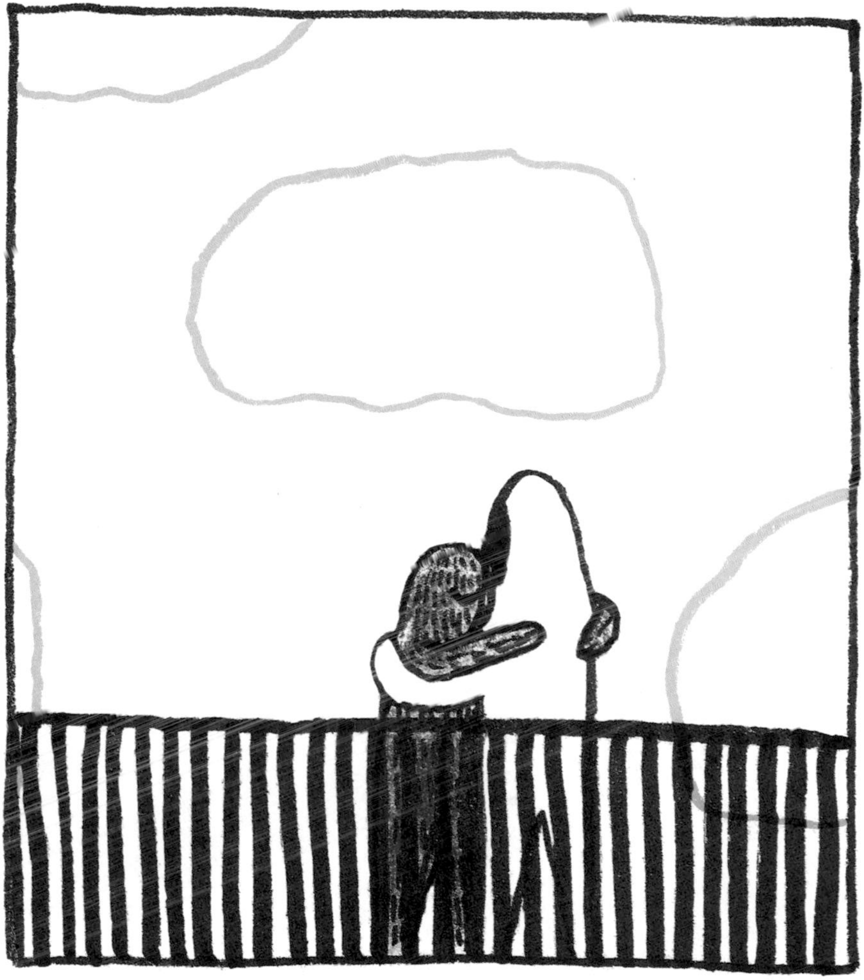

BUT NEVER SO
LONG THAT
IT BECOMES
A ROMANTIC
THING

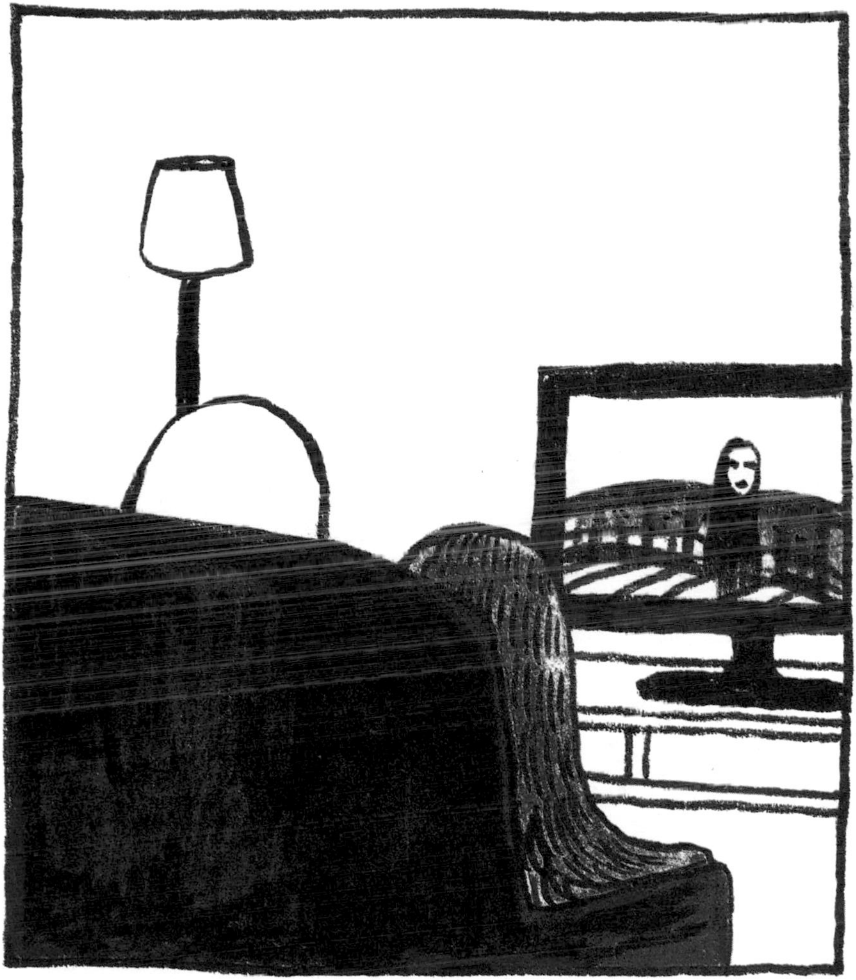

I WANT TO SIT ON
THE SAME COUCH
AND WATCH OUR
FAVORITE MOVIE
TOGETHER

AND MAYBE
LEAN IN TO
WHISPER OUR
FAVORITE LINES

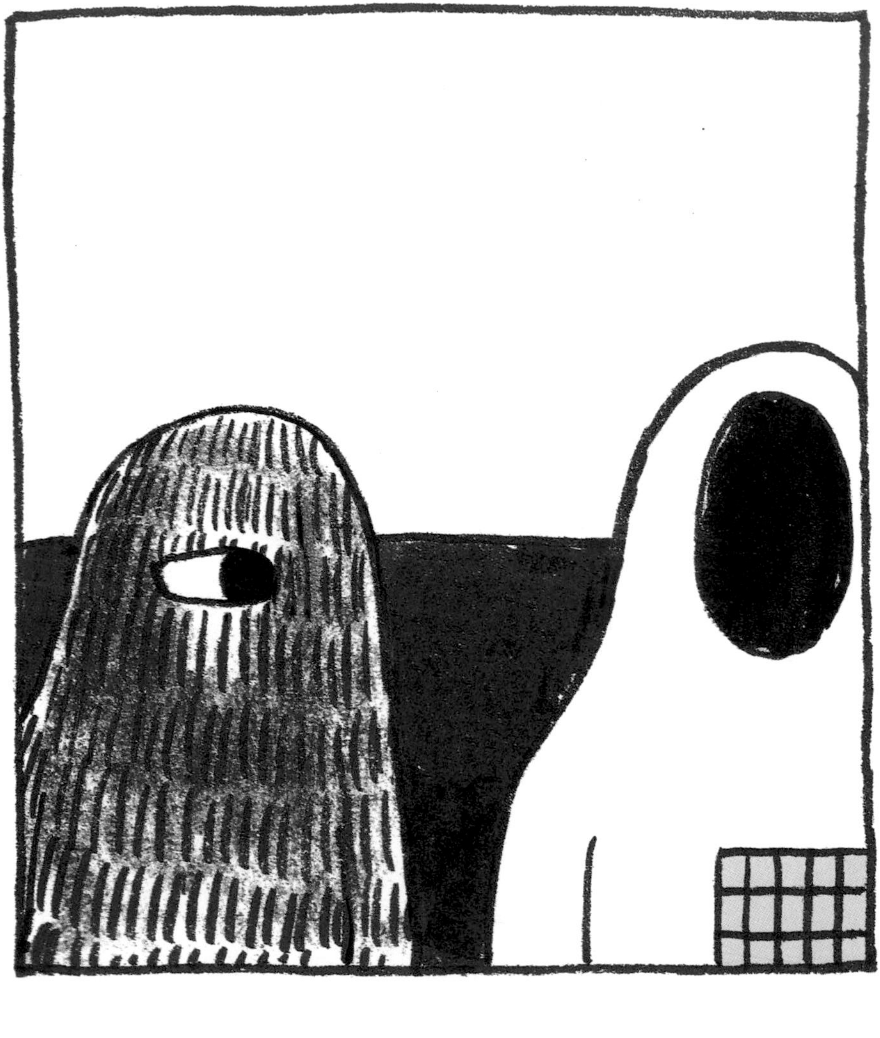

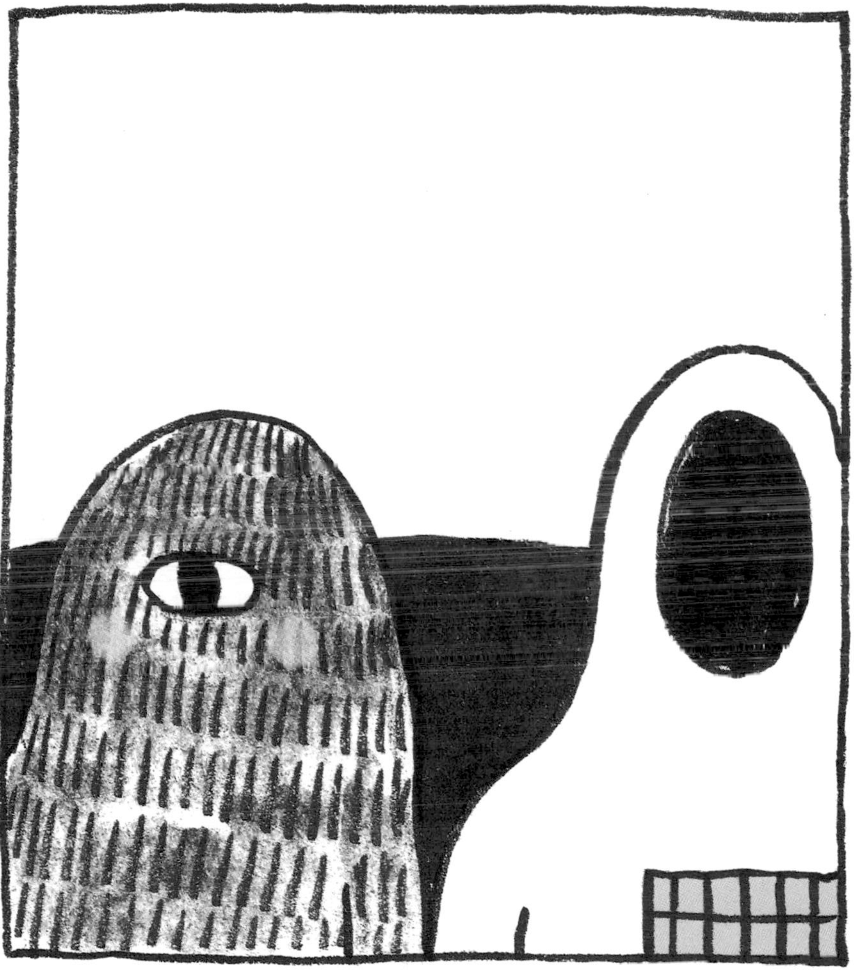

BUT NEVER WOULD
I PUT MY HEAD
ON YOUR SHOULDER
OR TRY TO HOLD
YOUR HAND.

BECAUSE THAT WOULD BE WEIRD.

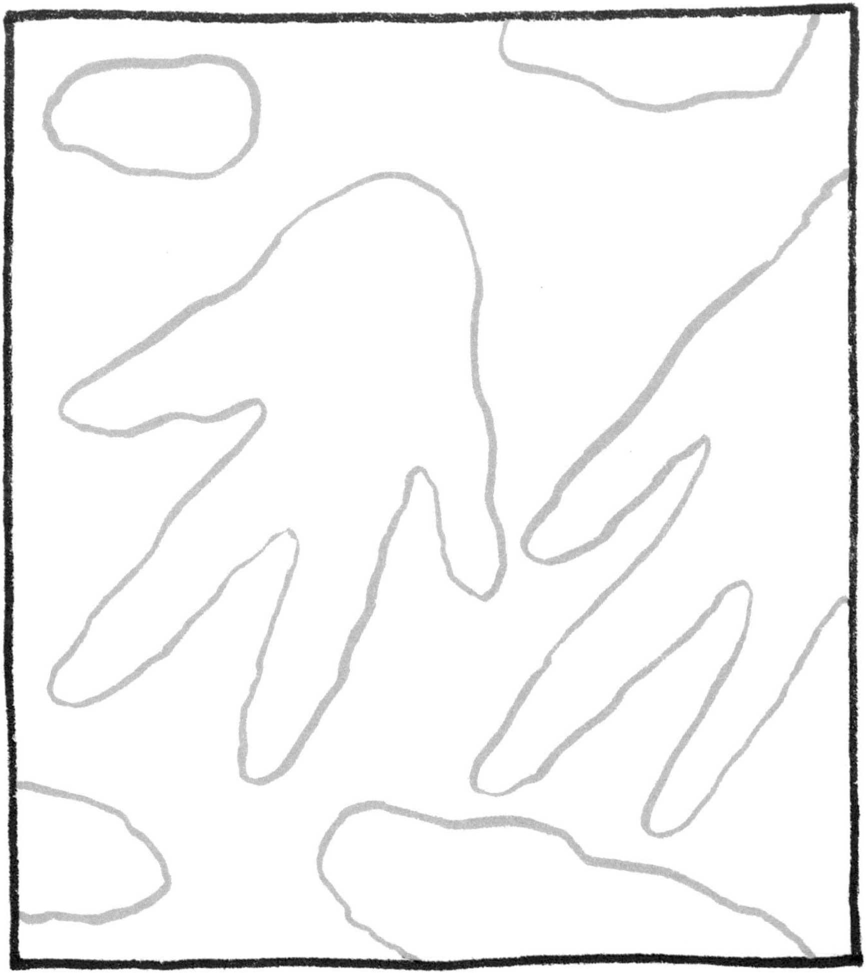

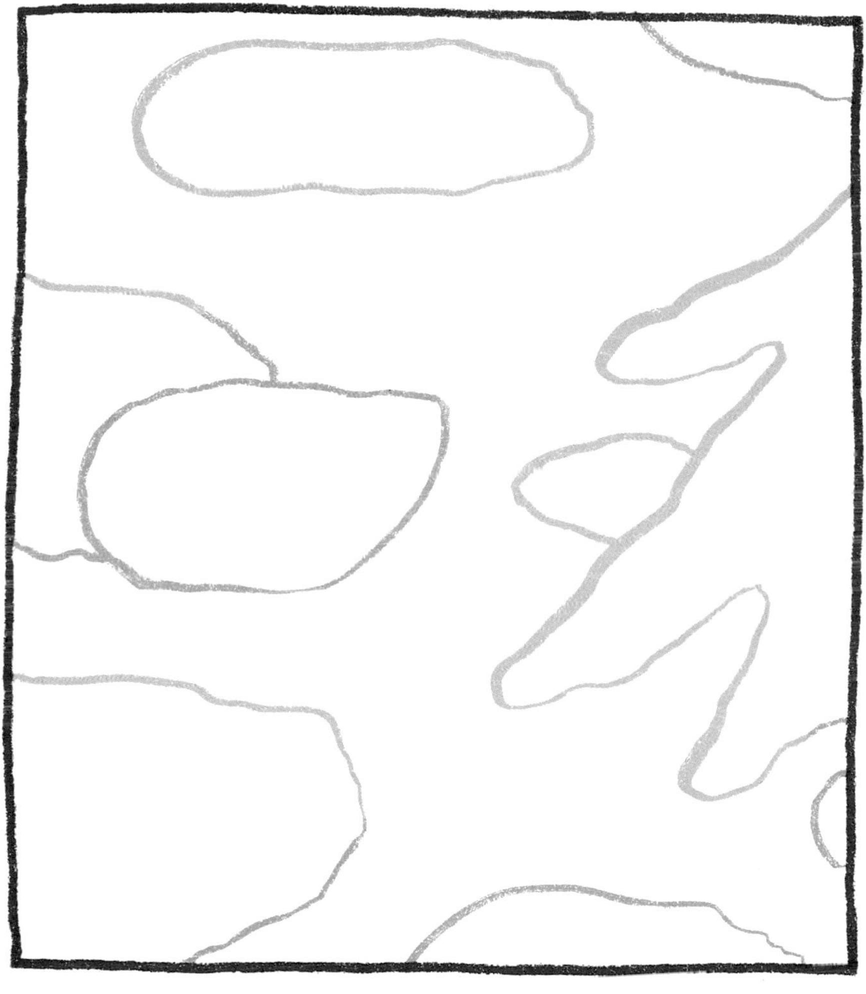

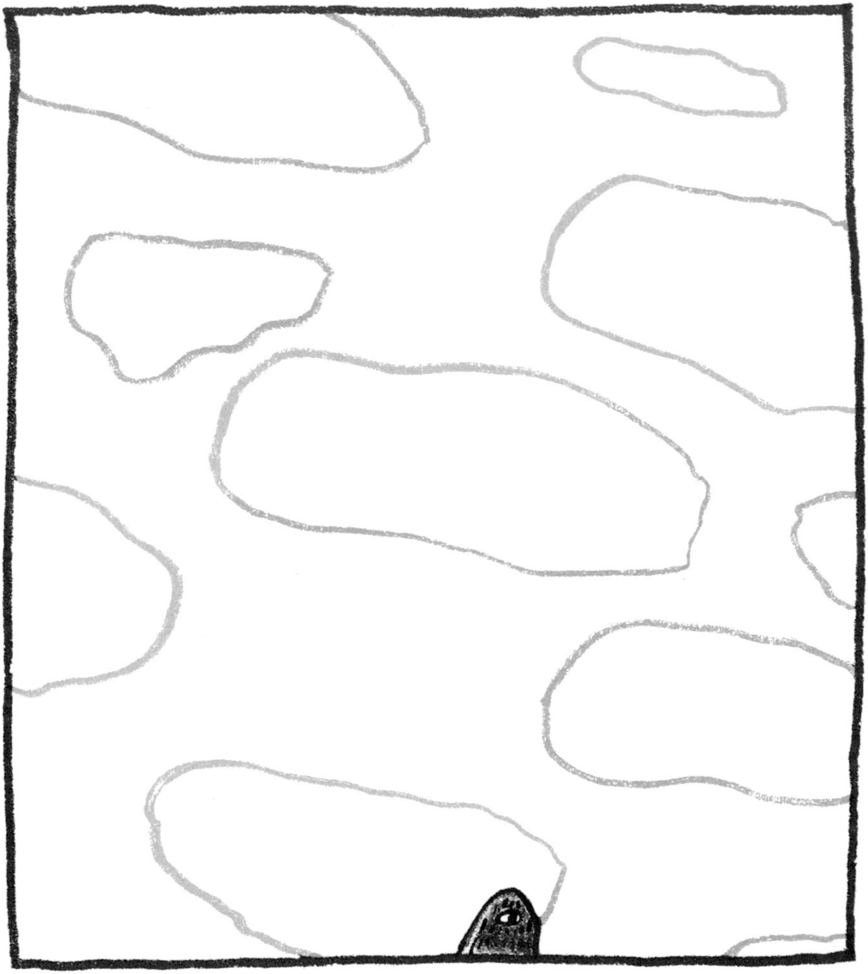

SO PLEASE,
BEFORE I
COMPLETELY
LOSE MY MIND,

CAN YOU
SURPRISE ME
WITH POKES
ON FACEBOOK?

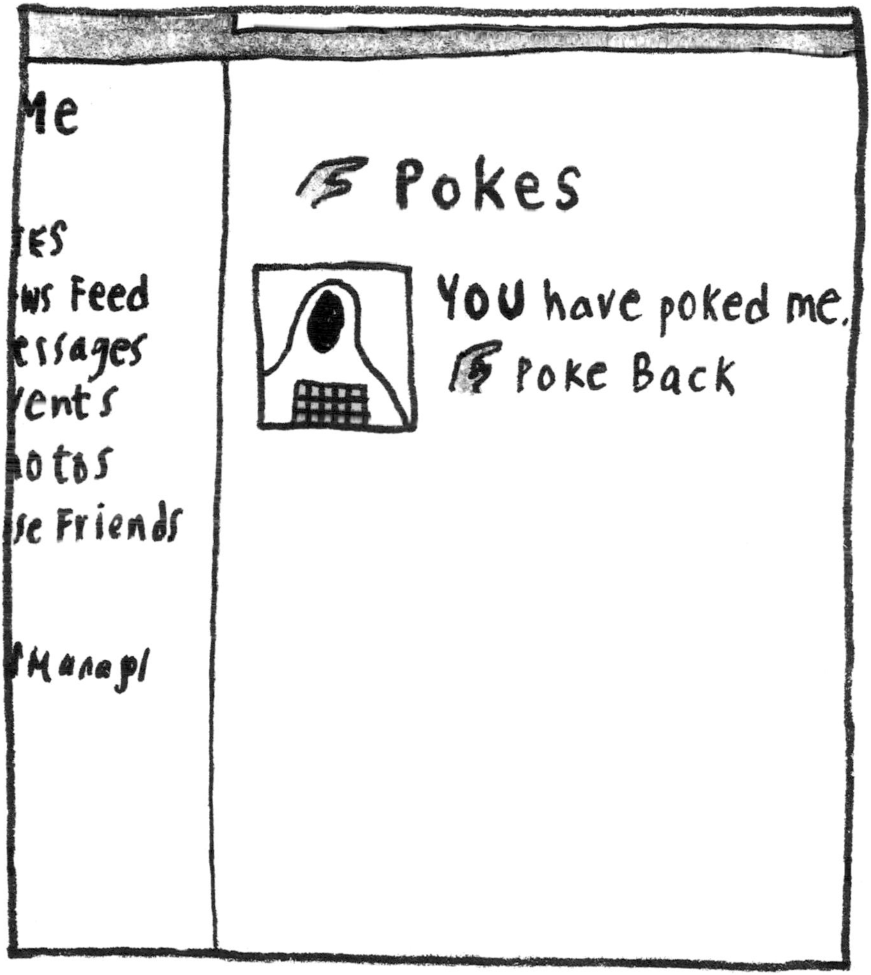
Me
Pokes
YOU have poked me.
Poke Back
es
ws Feed
essages
vents
otos
se Friends

CAN YOU RANDOMLY
E-MAIL ME WEIRD
BLOG LINKS THAT
REMIND YOU OF
ME?

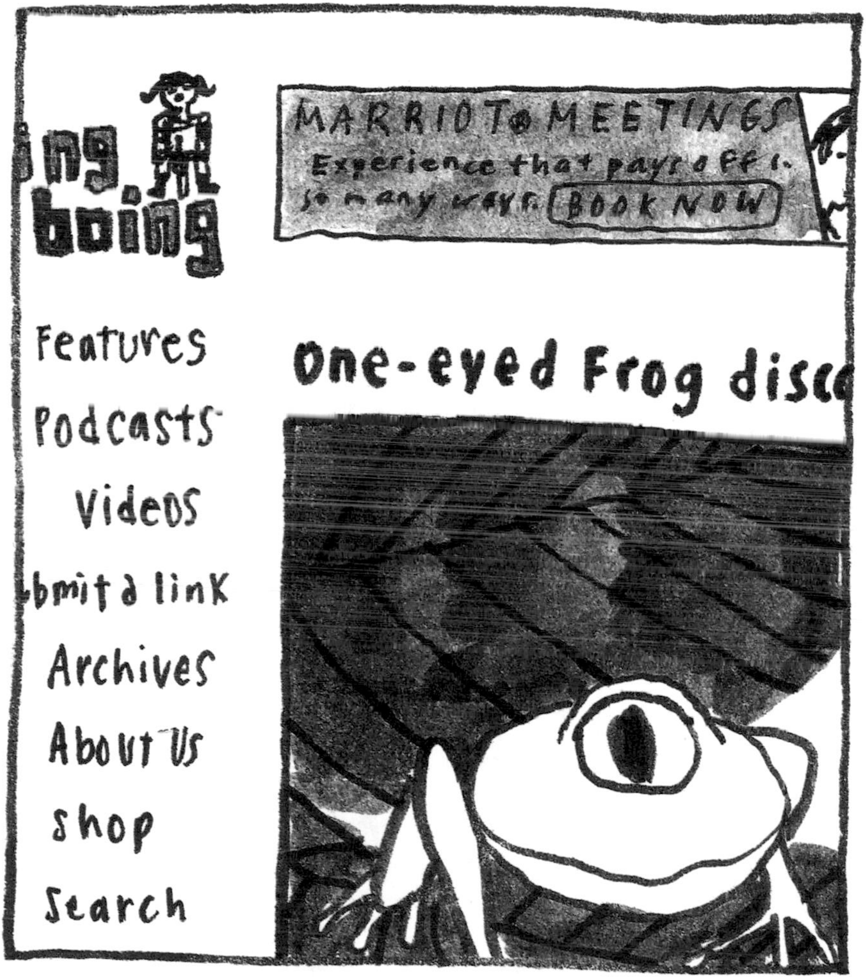

ing boing
MARRIOT® MEETINGS
Experience that pays off i.
so many ways. BOOK NOW
Features
Podcasts
Videos
bmit a link
Archives
About Us
Shop
Search
One-eyed Frog disc

CAN YOU TEXT ME WHEN SOMETHING CRAZY HAPPENS ON THE T.V. SHOW WE ARE BOTH WATCHING?

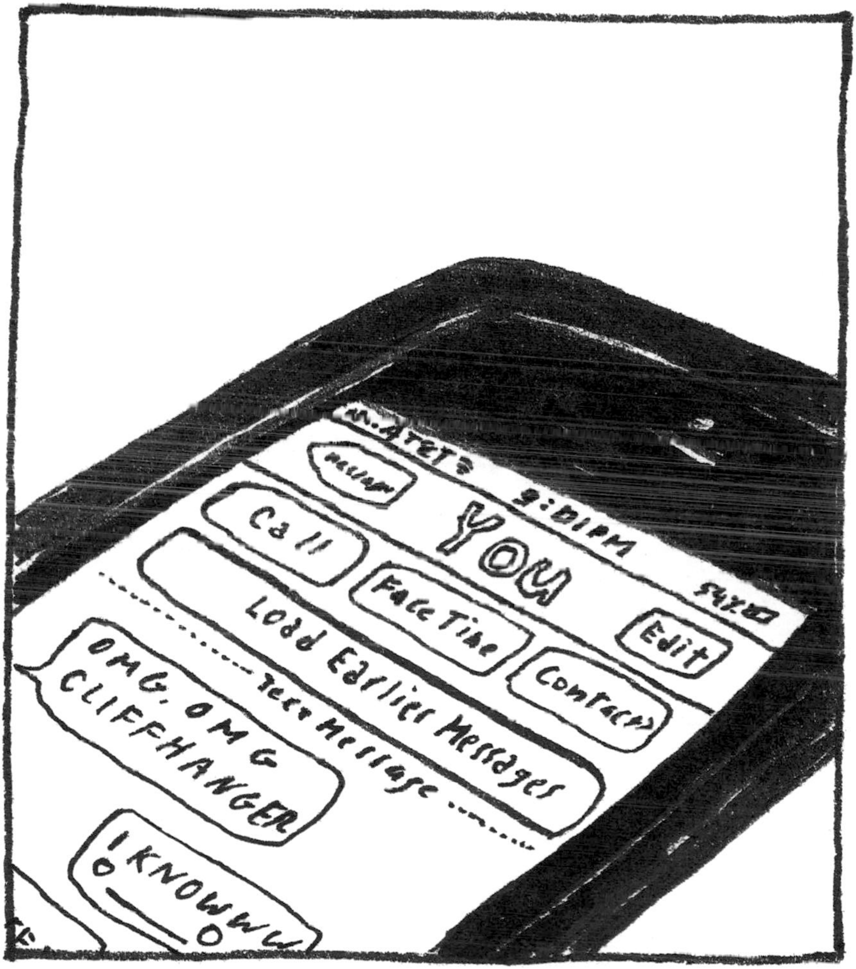

AT&T
9:01PM
YOU
Call
FaceTime
Contact
Edit
Load Earlier Messages
Text Message
OMG, OMG OMG CLIFFHANGER
I KNOWWWW

AND LET ME
WALK WITH
YOU TO YOUR
FAVORITE FOOD
TRUCK?

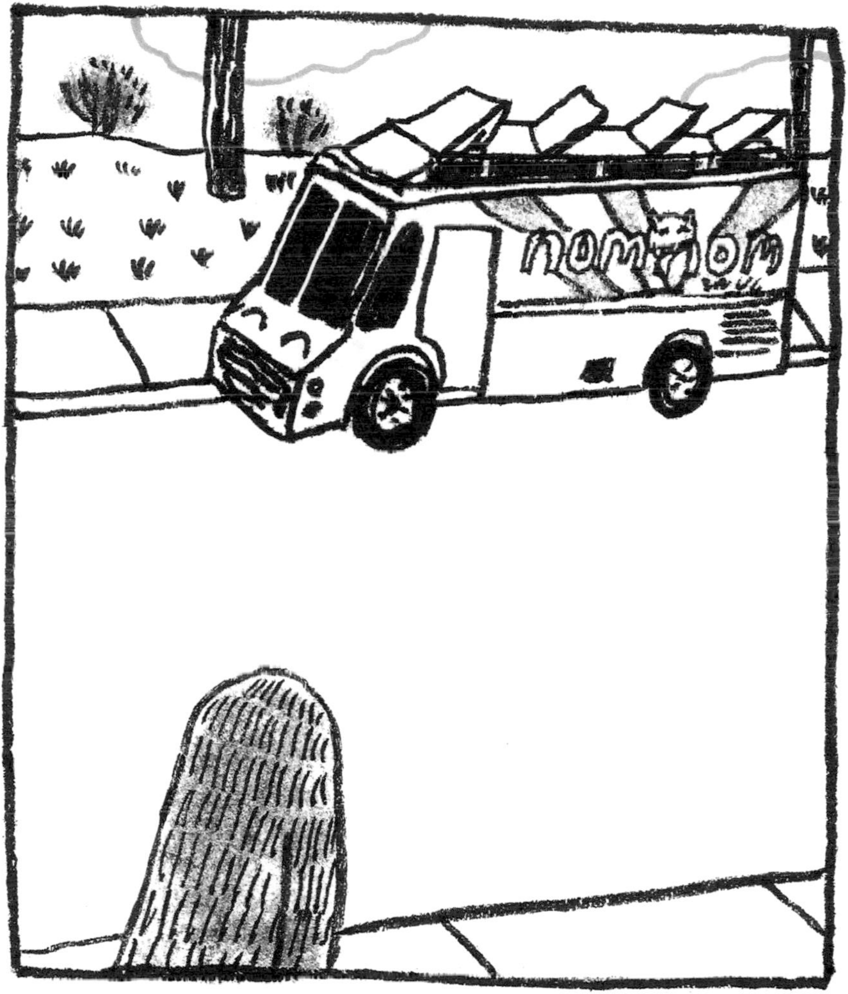
nom om

IN RETURN, I
WILL LAUGH AT
ALL YOUR JOKES
(EVEN THE
UNFUNNY ONES)

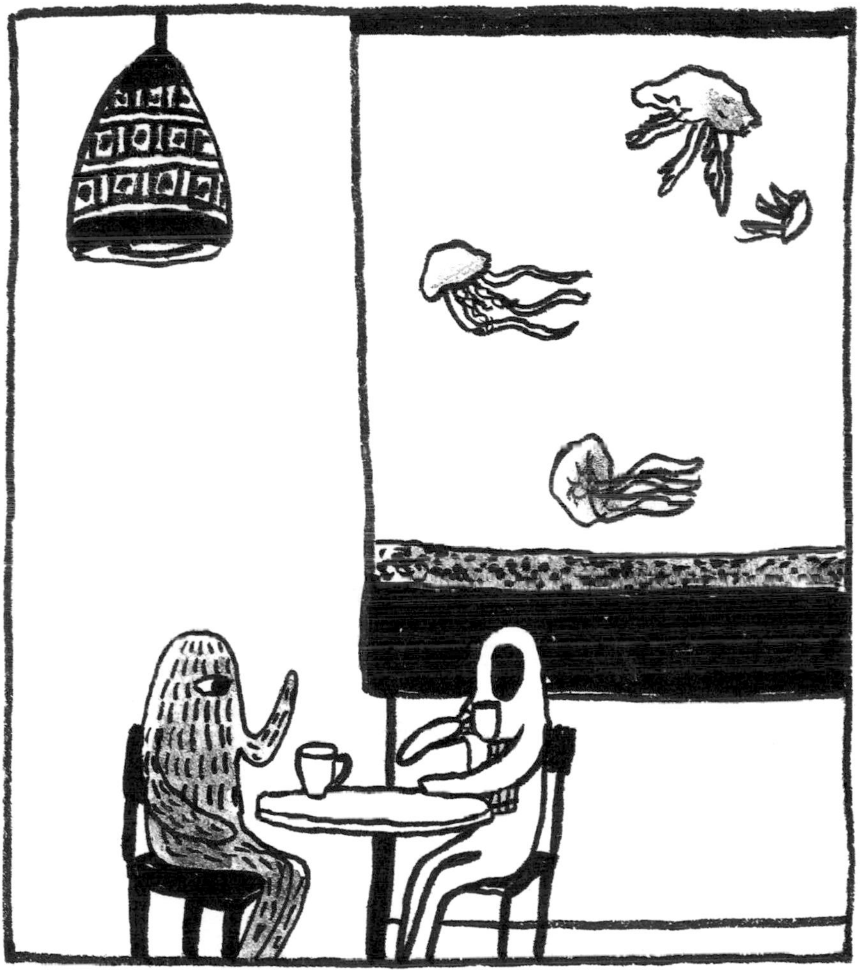

AND FIND THE
BEST HOLE-IN-
THE-WALL CAFES
FOR US TO HAVE
NEVER-ENDING
CONVERSATIONS
IN.

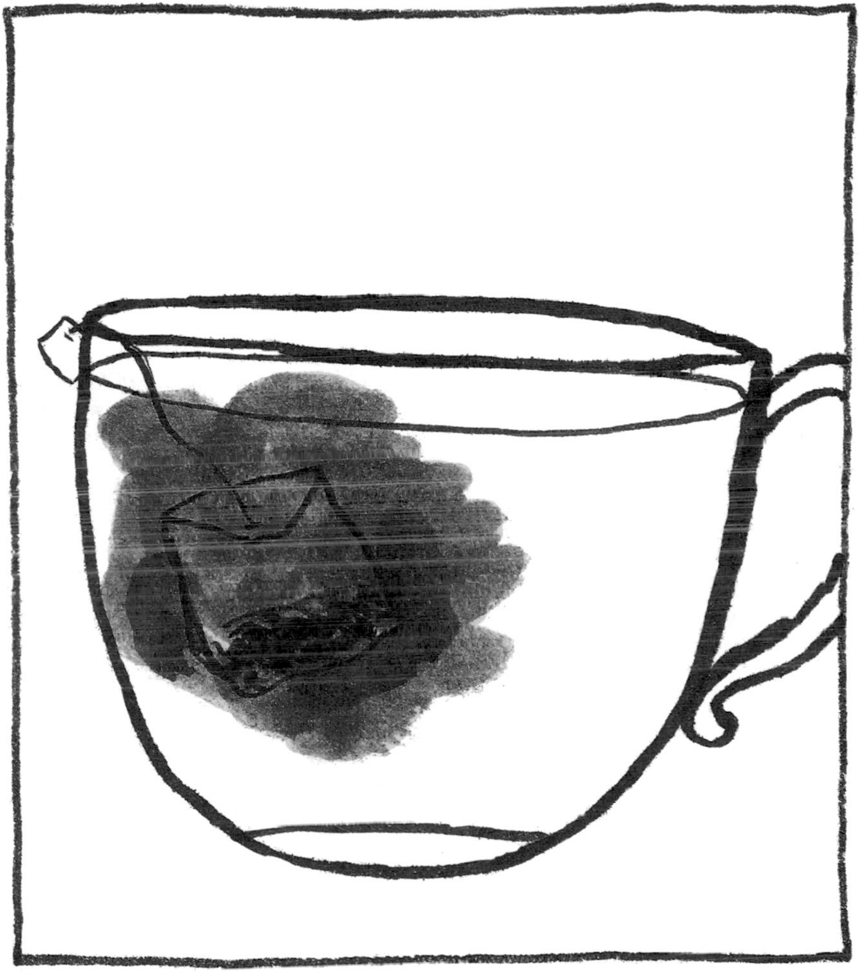

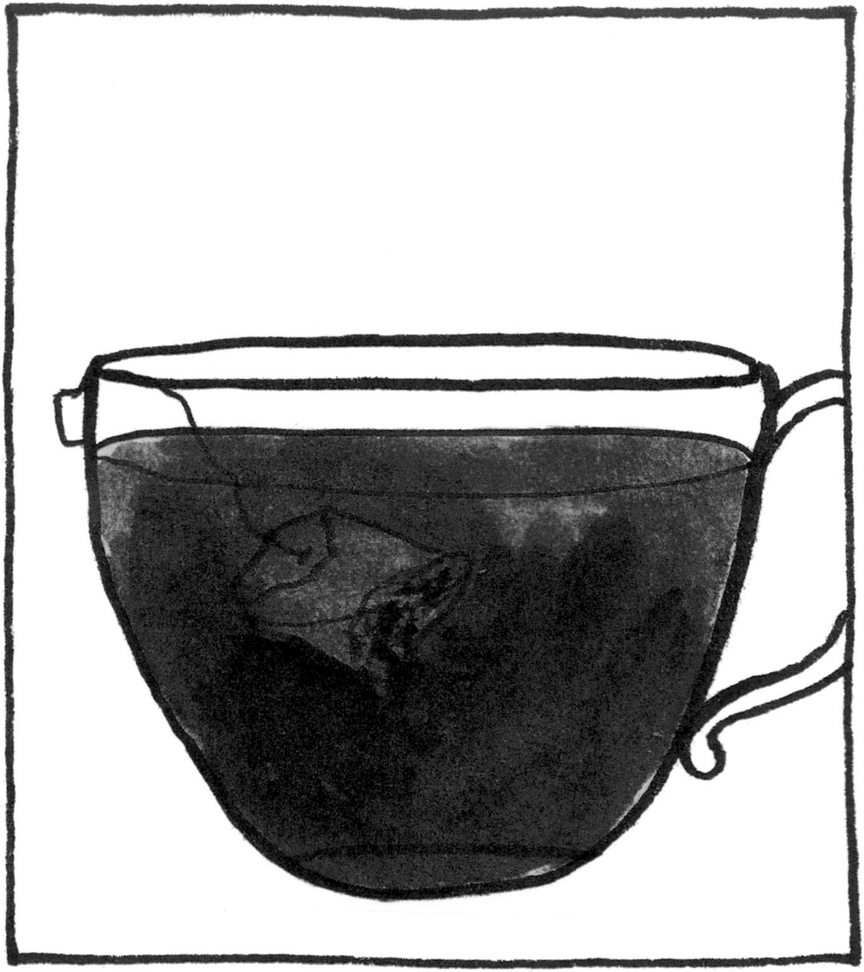

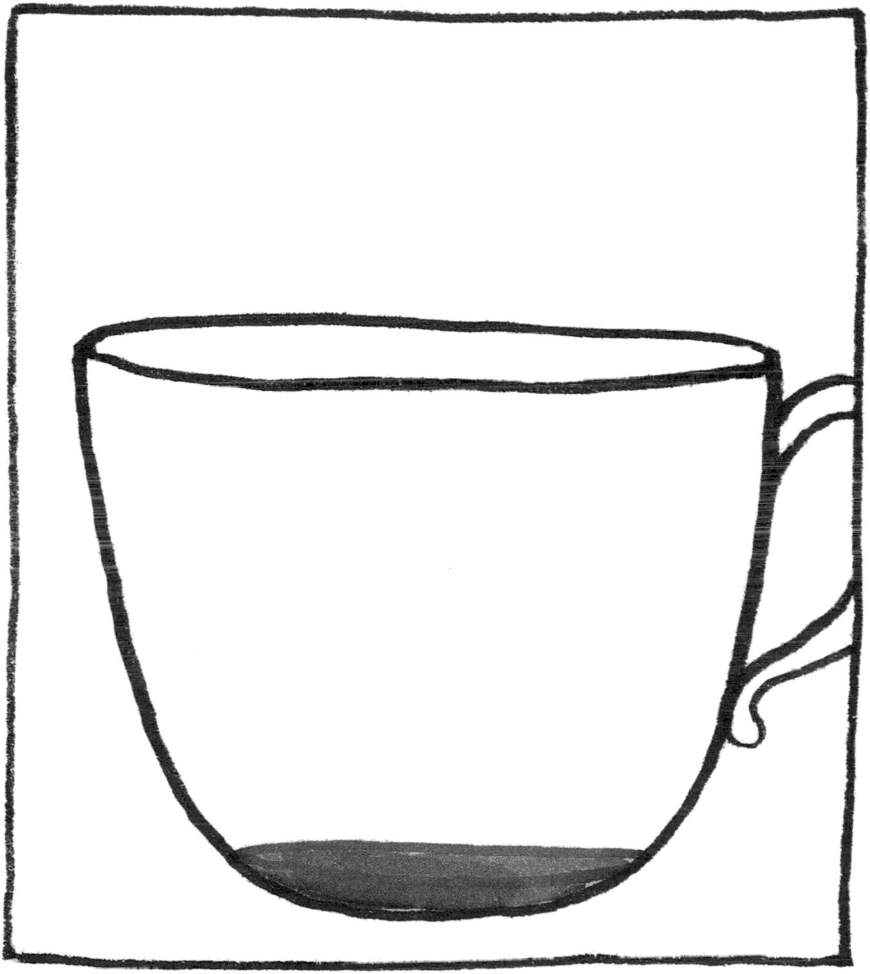

I WILL MAKE BAD PHOTOSHOP DRAWINGS COMMEMORATING OUR HANG-OUTS

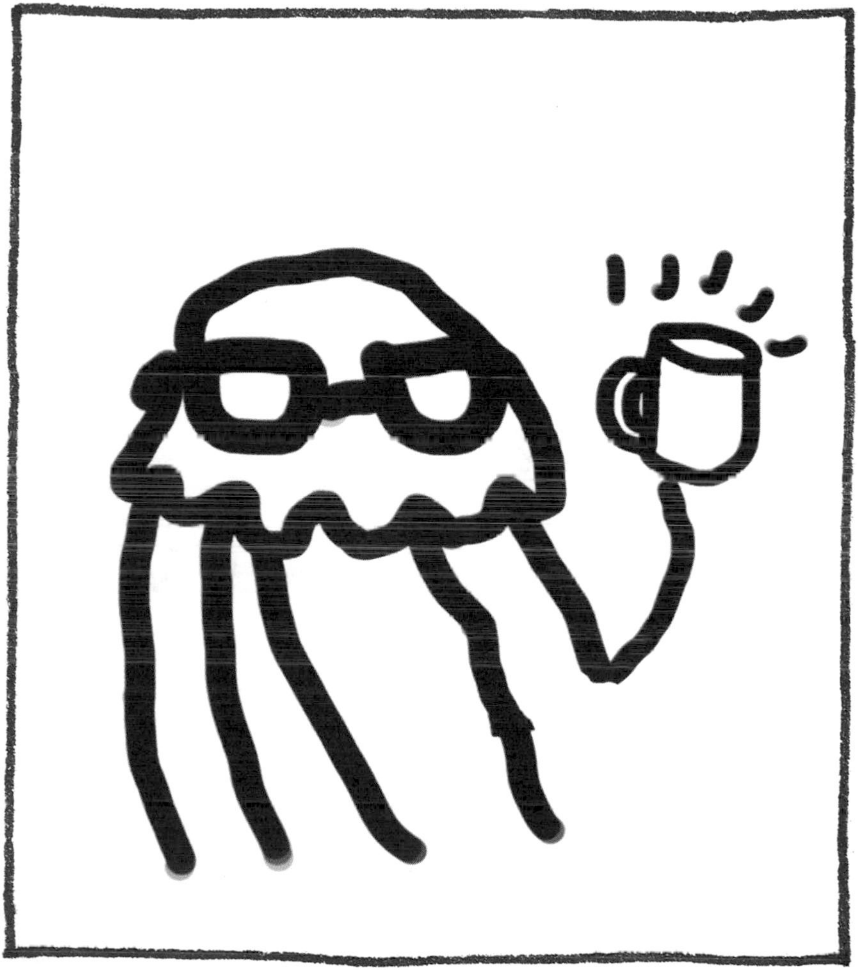

AND EVERY
SINGLE ONE
OF OUR
INTERNET MEME
CAT JOKES

WILL BE
REFERENCED
IN THE BIRTHDAY
CARDS I WILL
DRAW FOR YOU
EVERY YEAR.

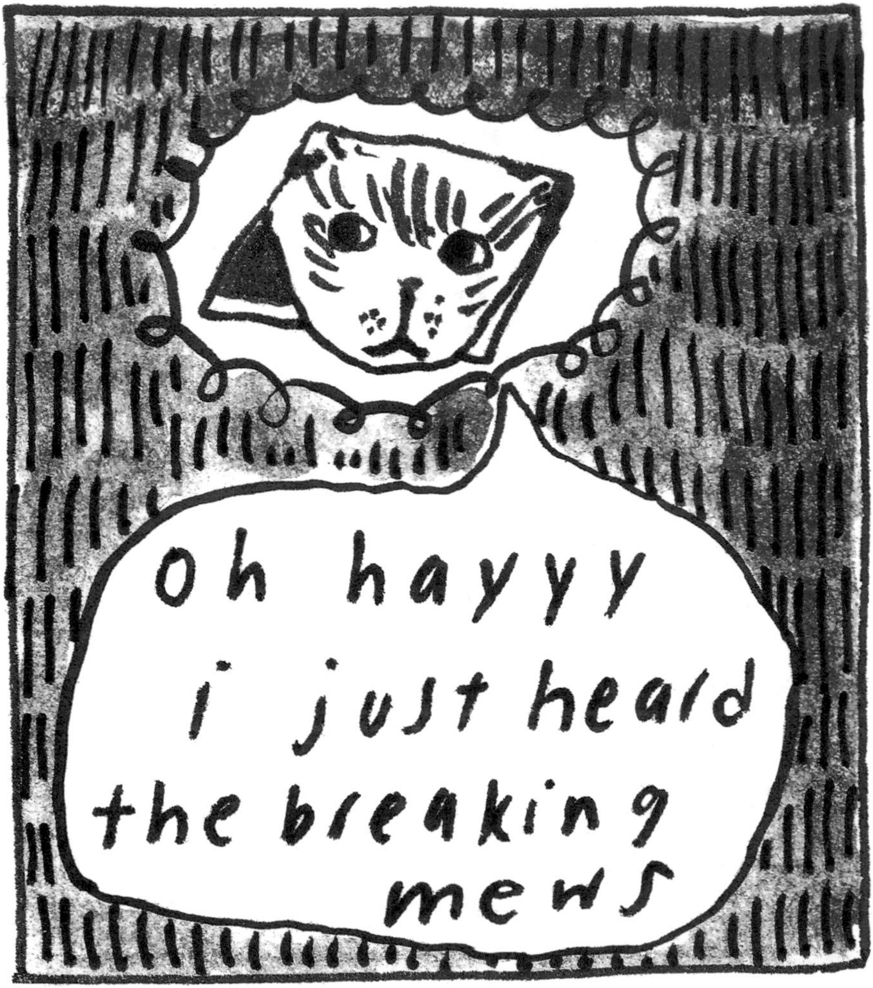
oh hayyy i just heard the breaking mews

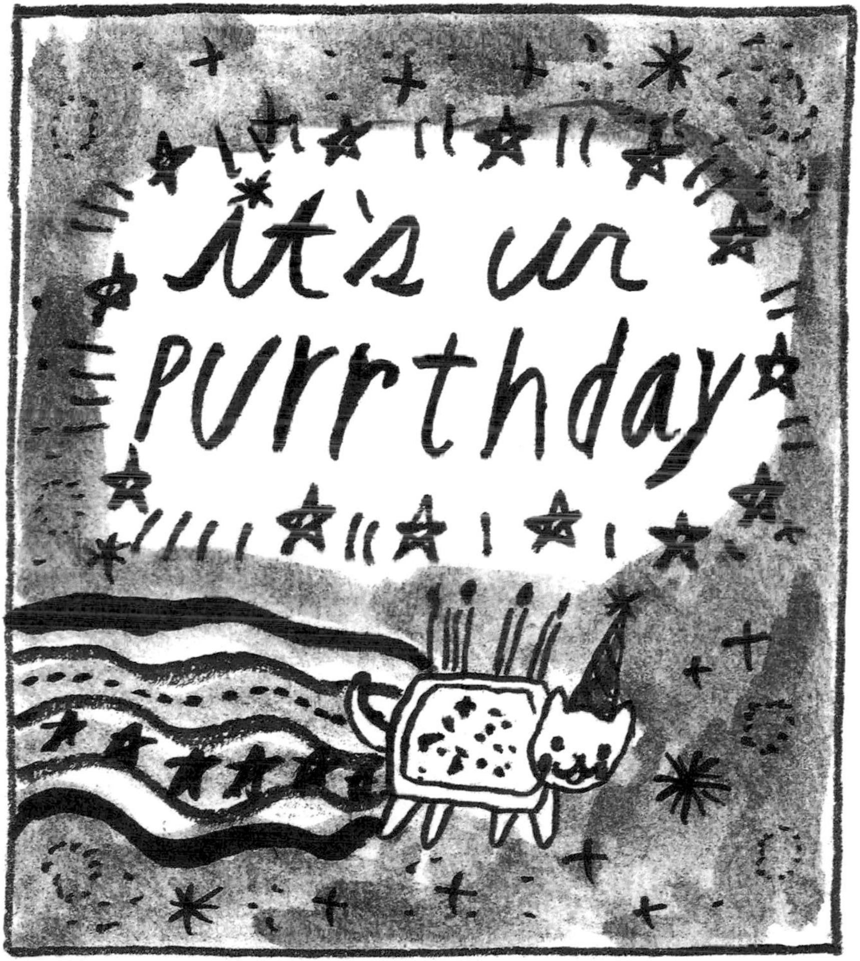
it's ur purrthday

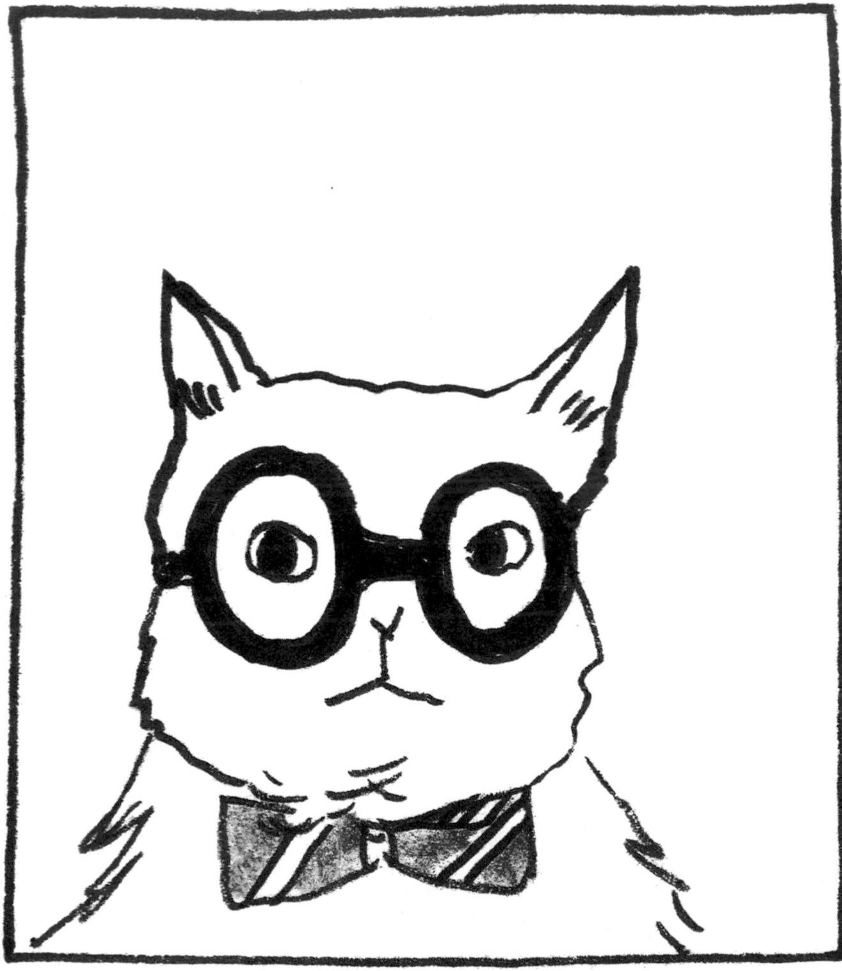

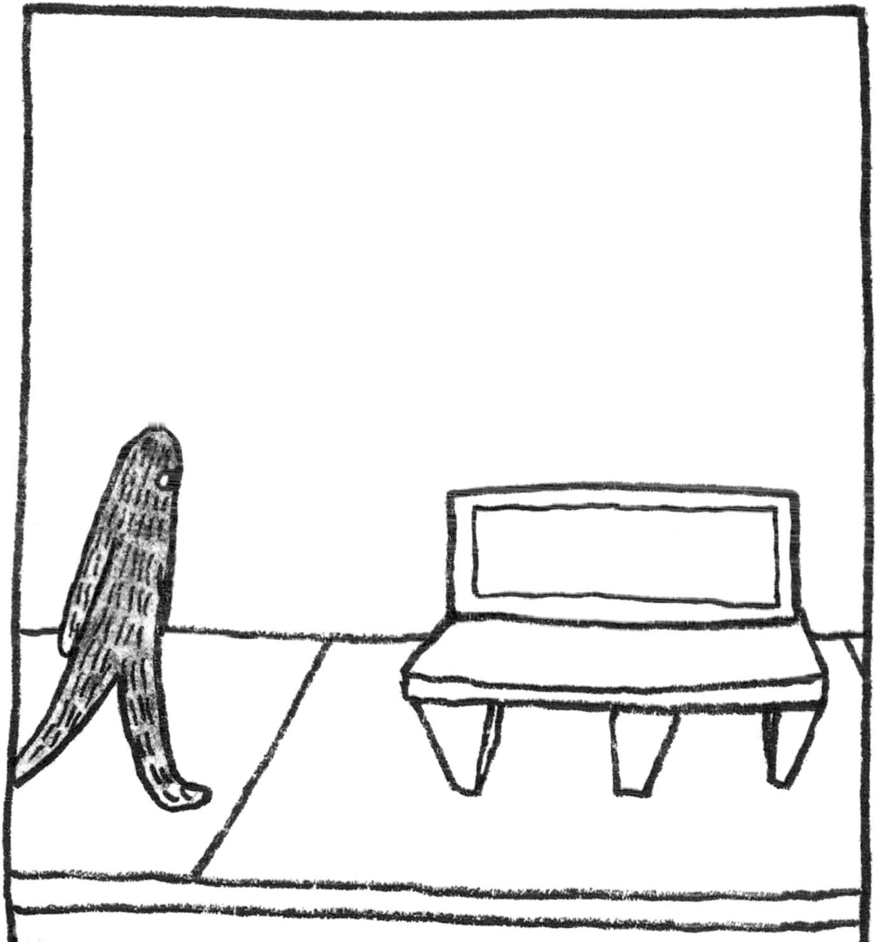

BELIEVE IT OR
NOT, I WOULDN'T
BE SAD IF YOU
ARE ALREADY
IN A ROMANTIC
RELATIONSHIP.

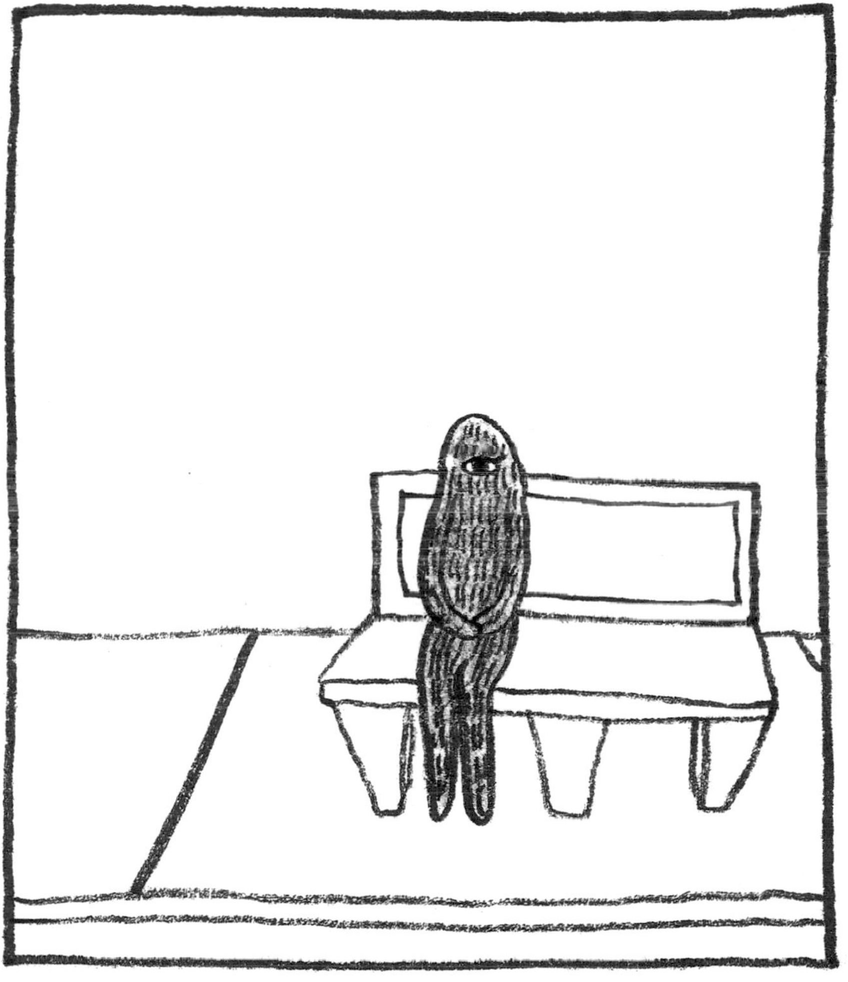

AS A MATTER
OF FACT, I
WOULD BE
REALLY HAPPY
FOR YOU

BECAUSE THAT'S WHAT FRIENDS ARE FOR.

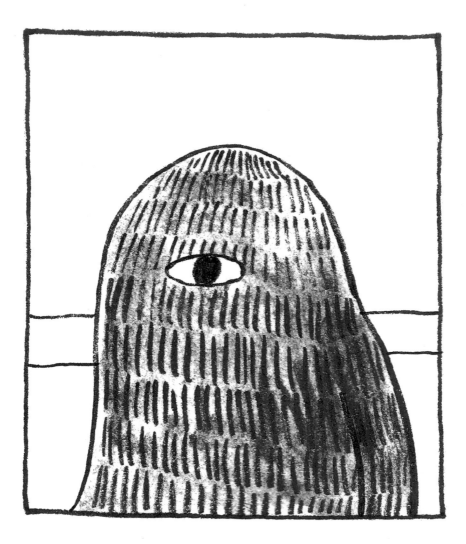

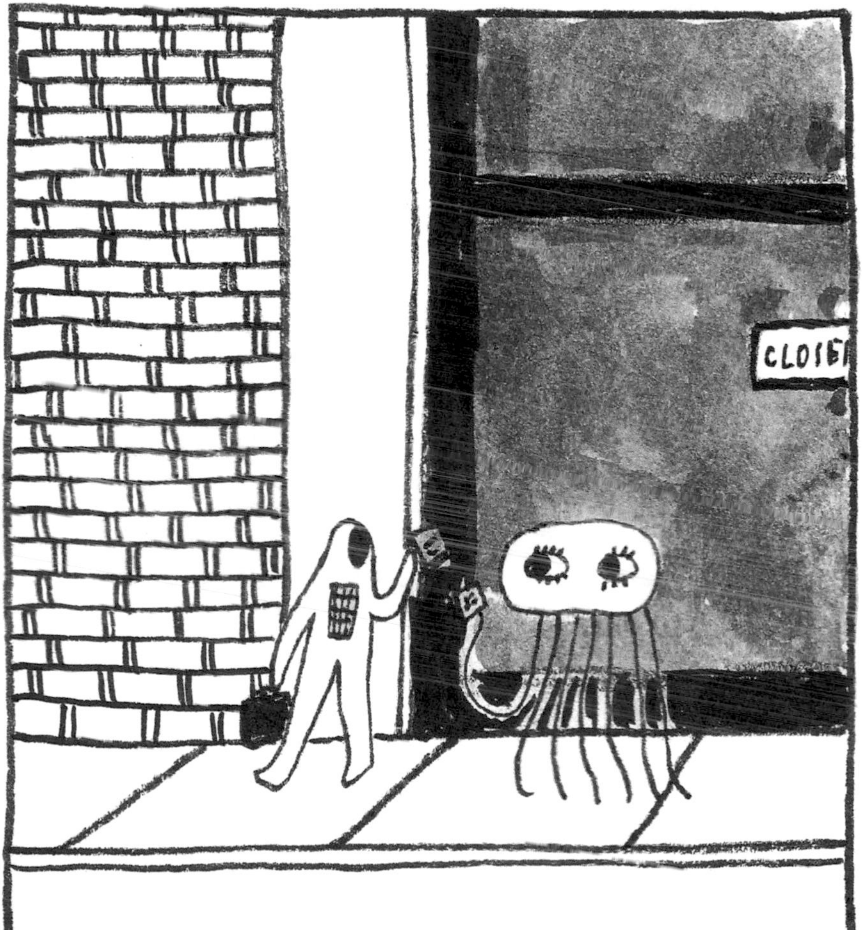
CLOSE

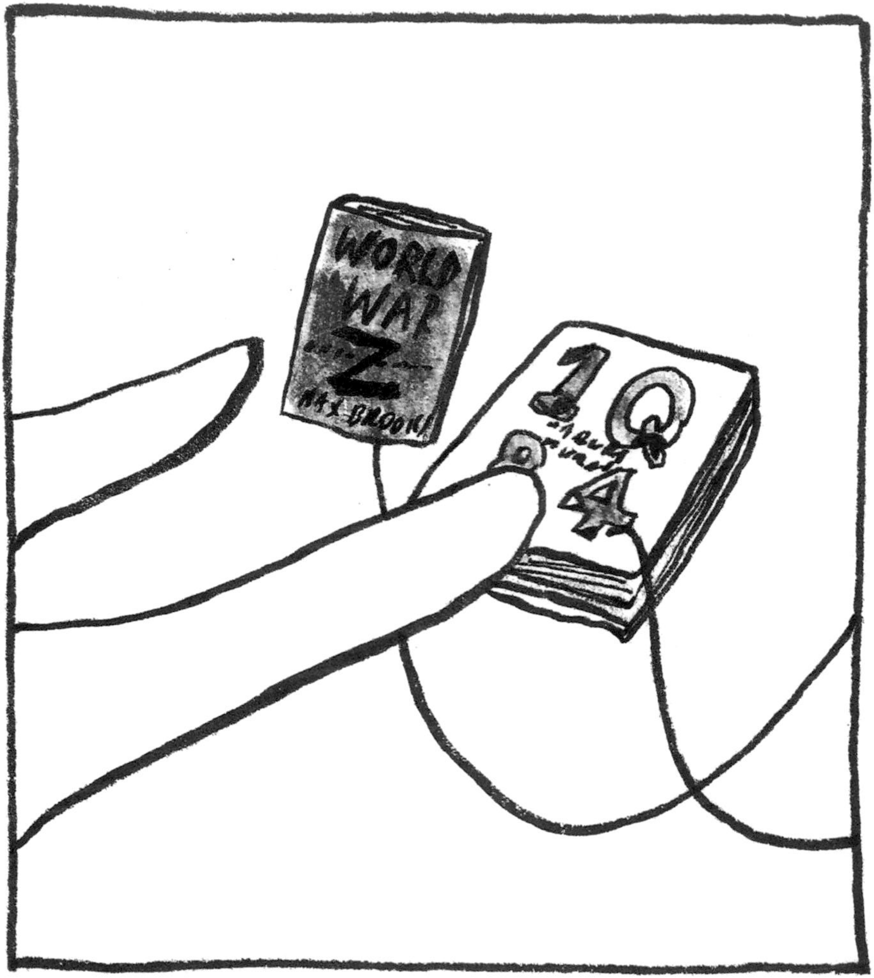
WORLD WAR Z
MAX BROOKS

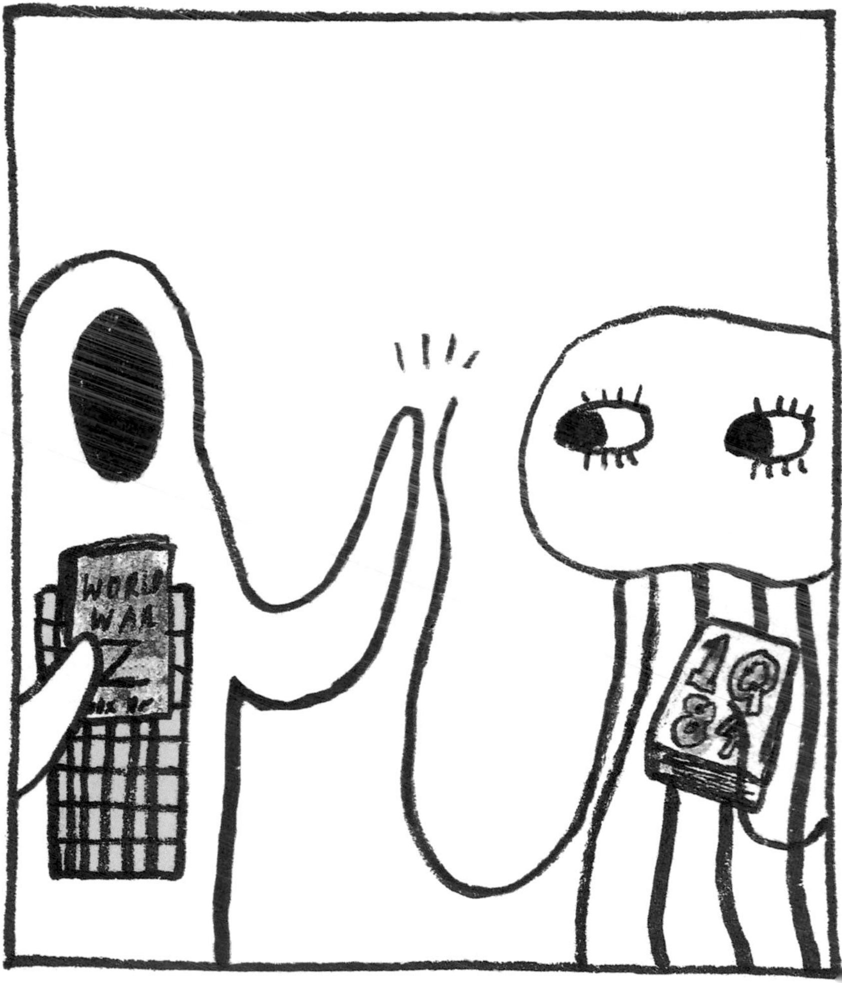
WORLD WAR Z
1984

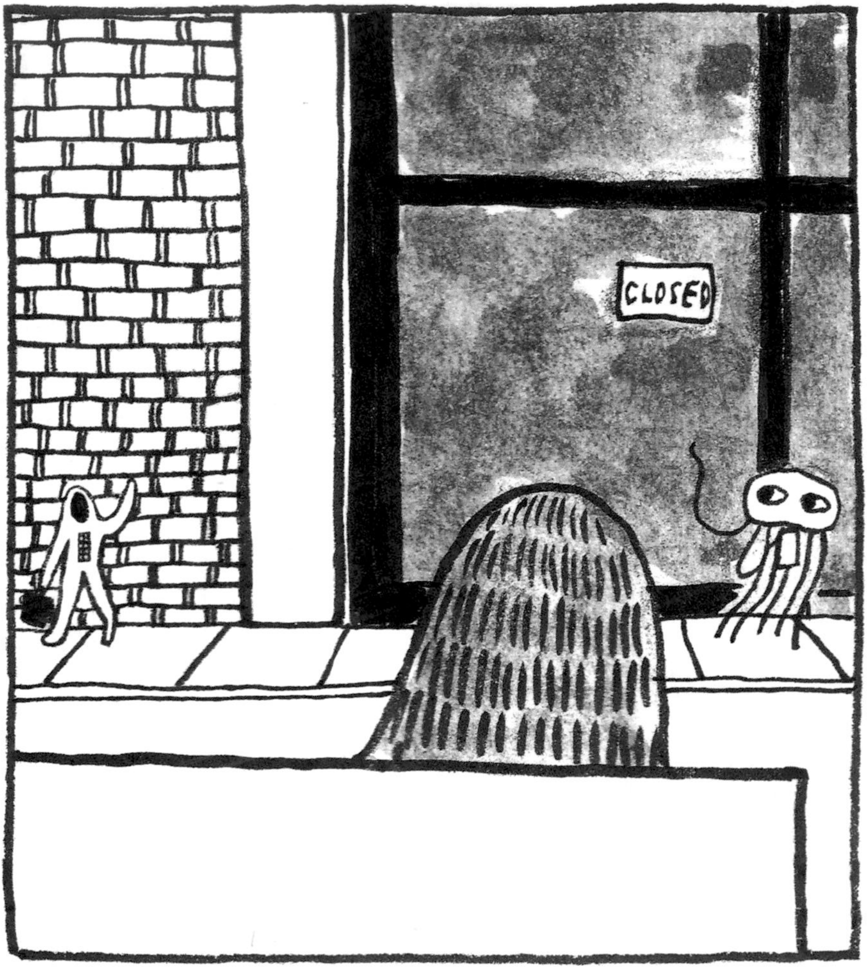
CLOSED

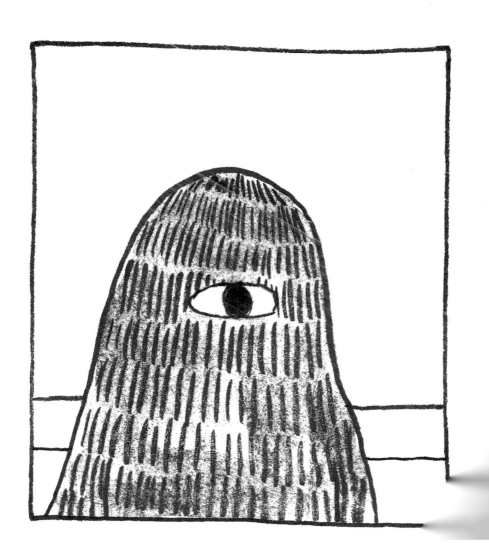

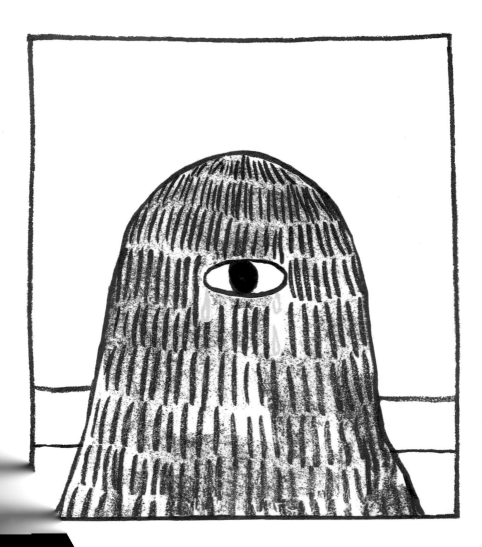

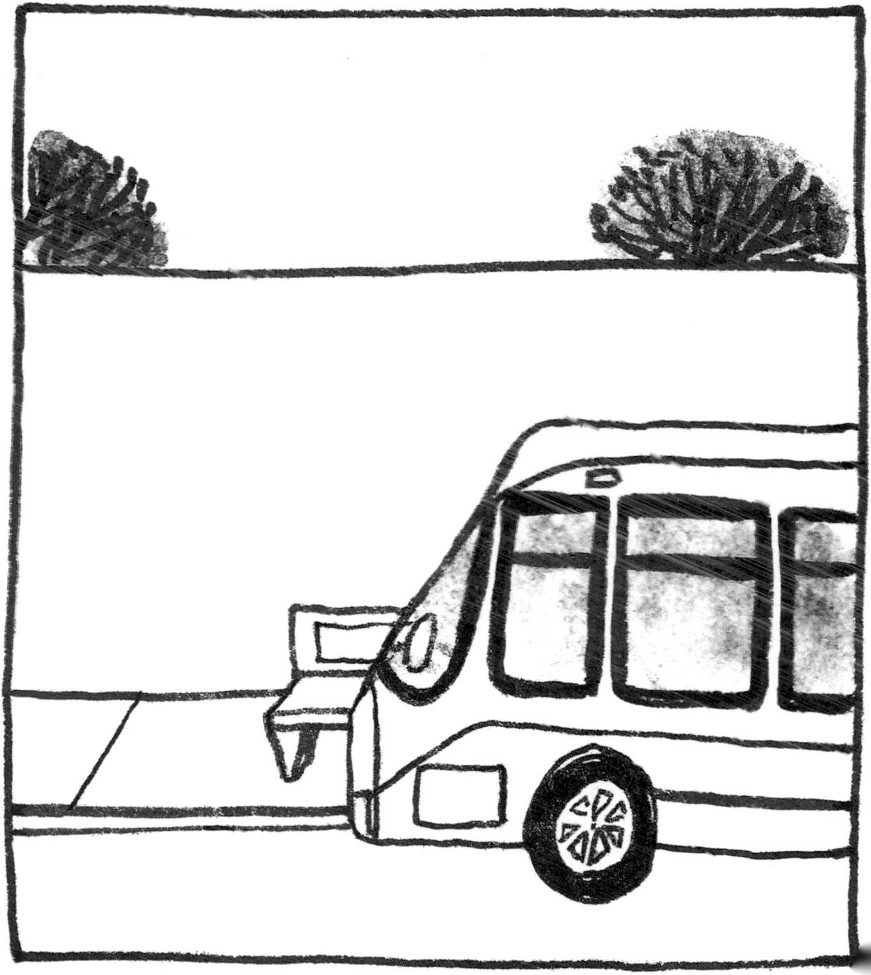

BUT IF YOUR
SUPER-AWESOME
CLOSE FRIEND
QUOTA HAS
ALREADY REACHED
ITS CAPACITY

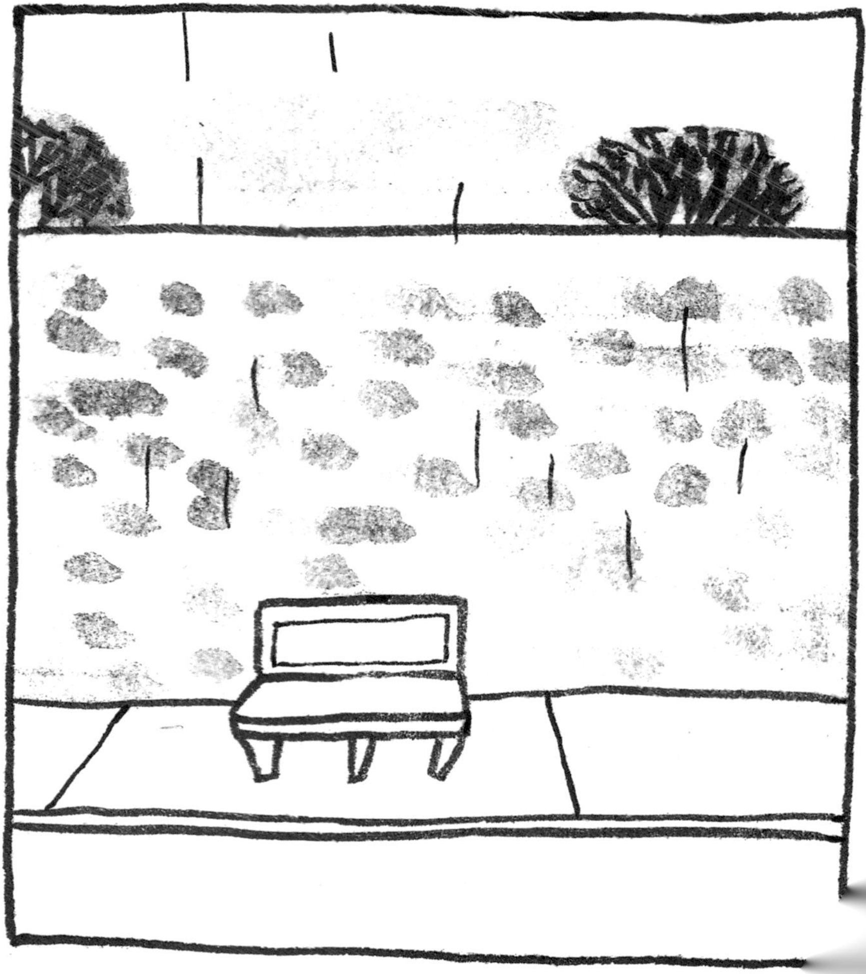

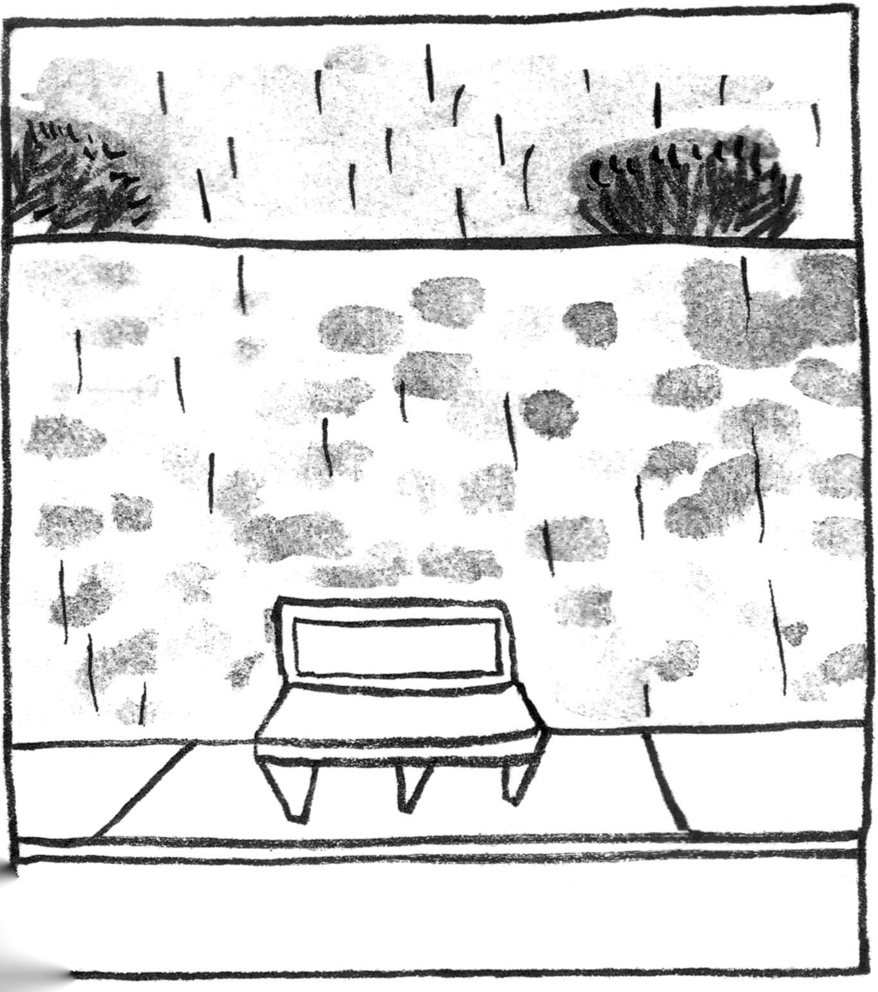

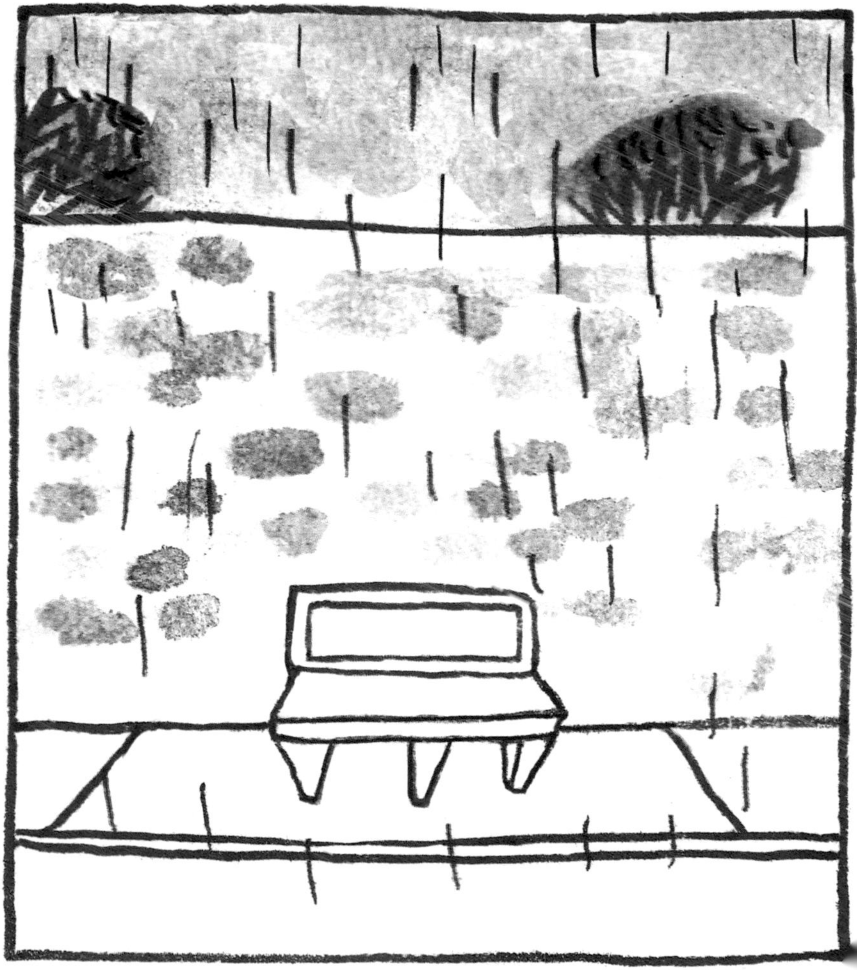

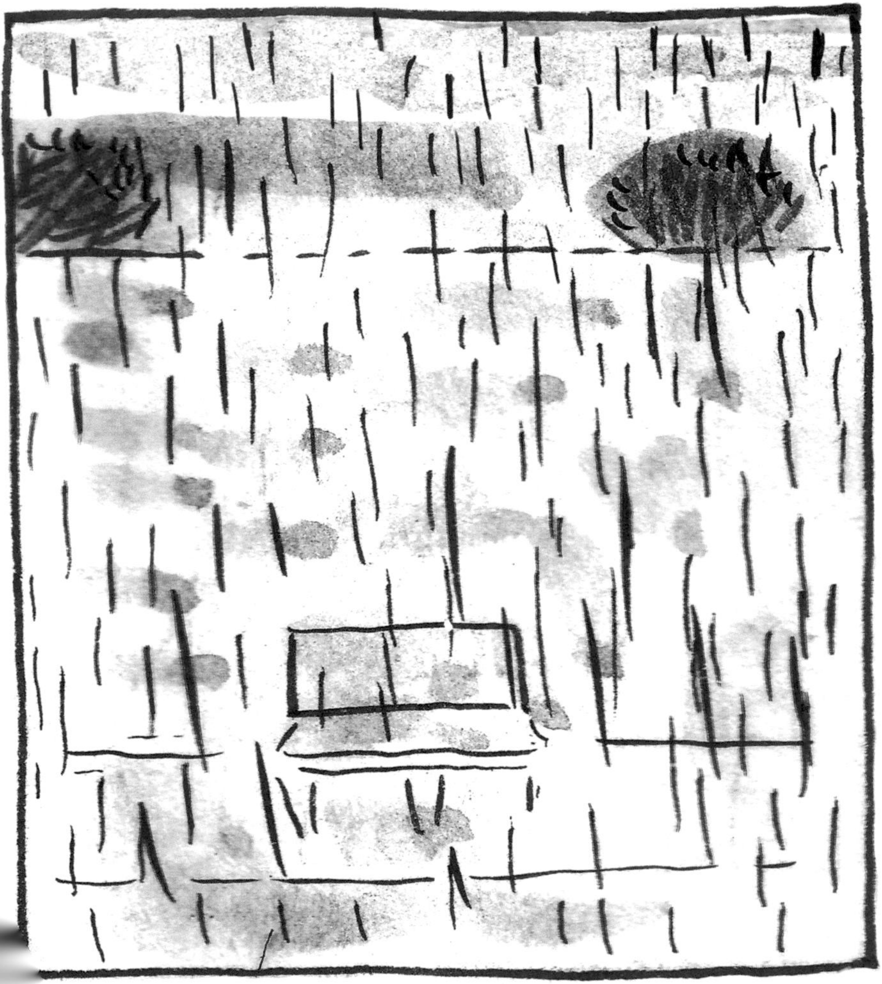

THEN THAT
WOULD REALLY
BREAK MY FRIEND
HEART INTO A
MILLION PIECES.

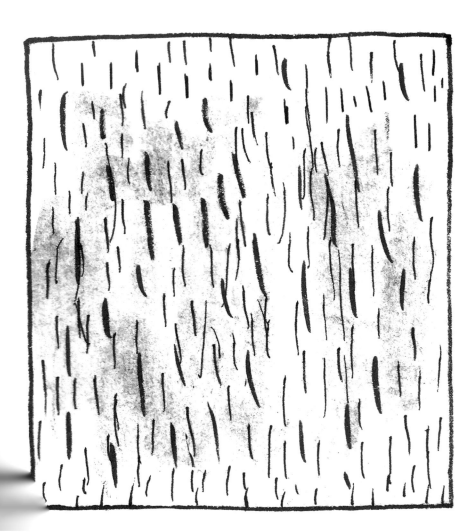

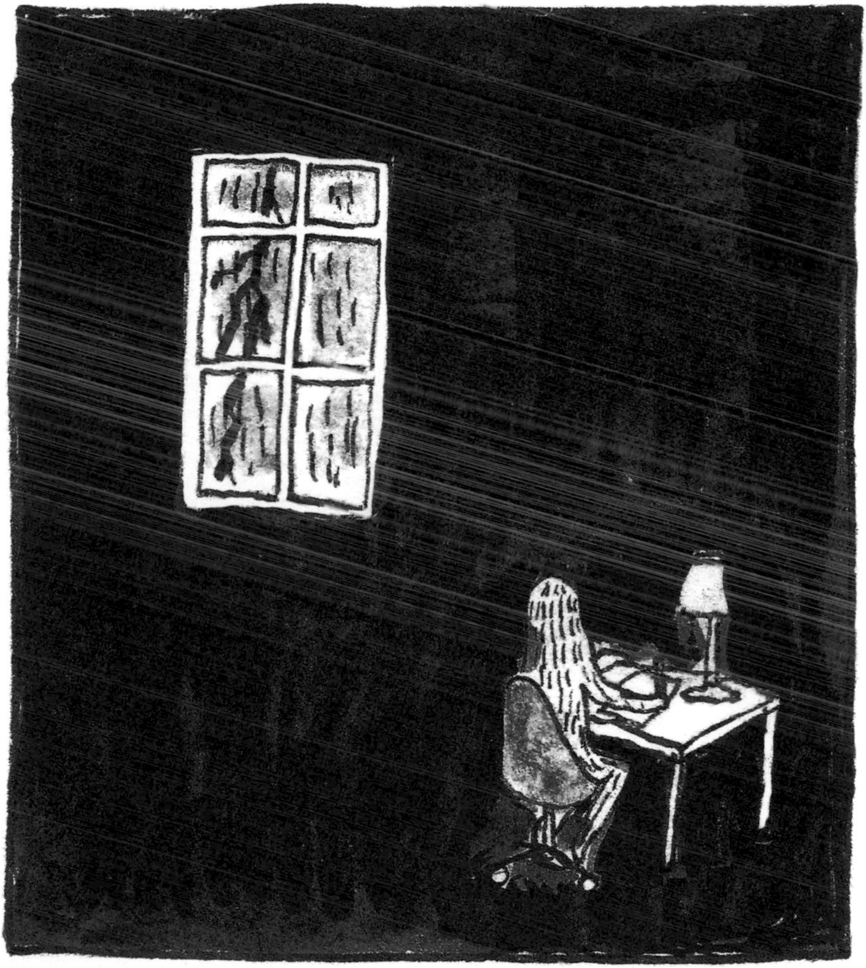

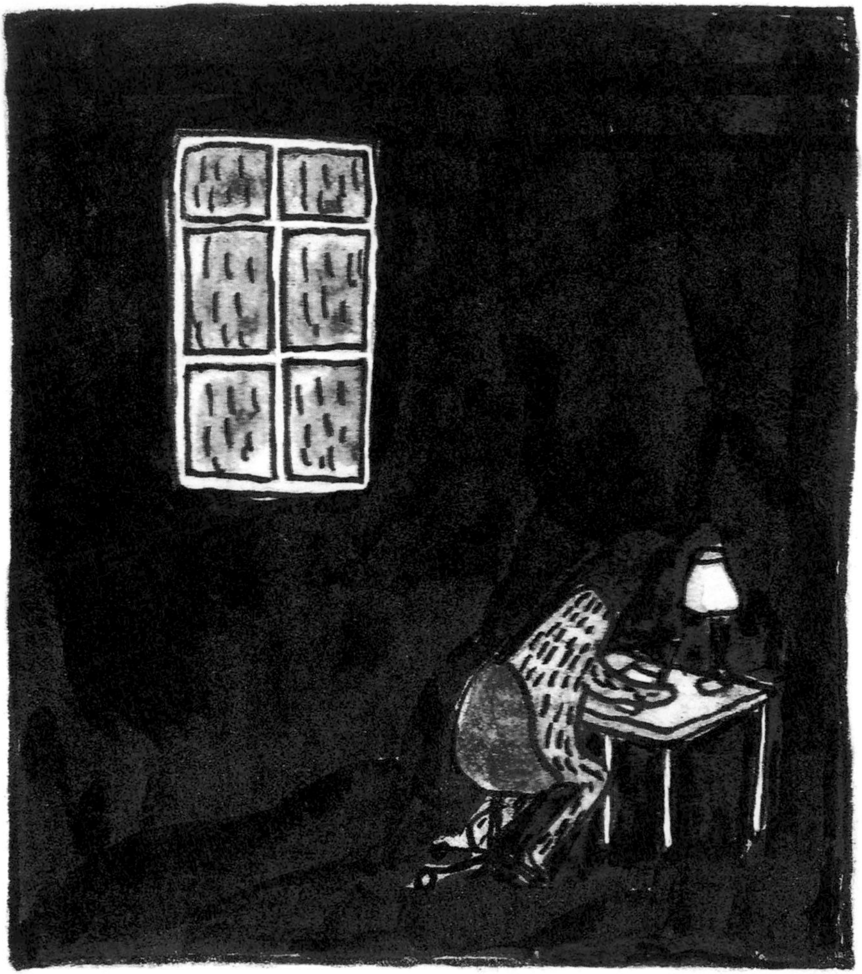

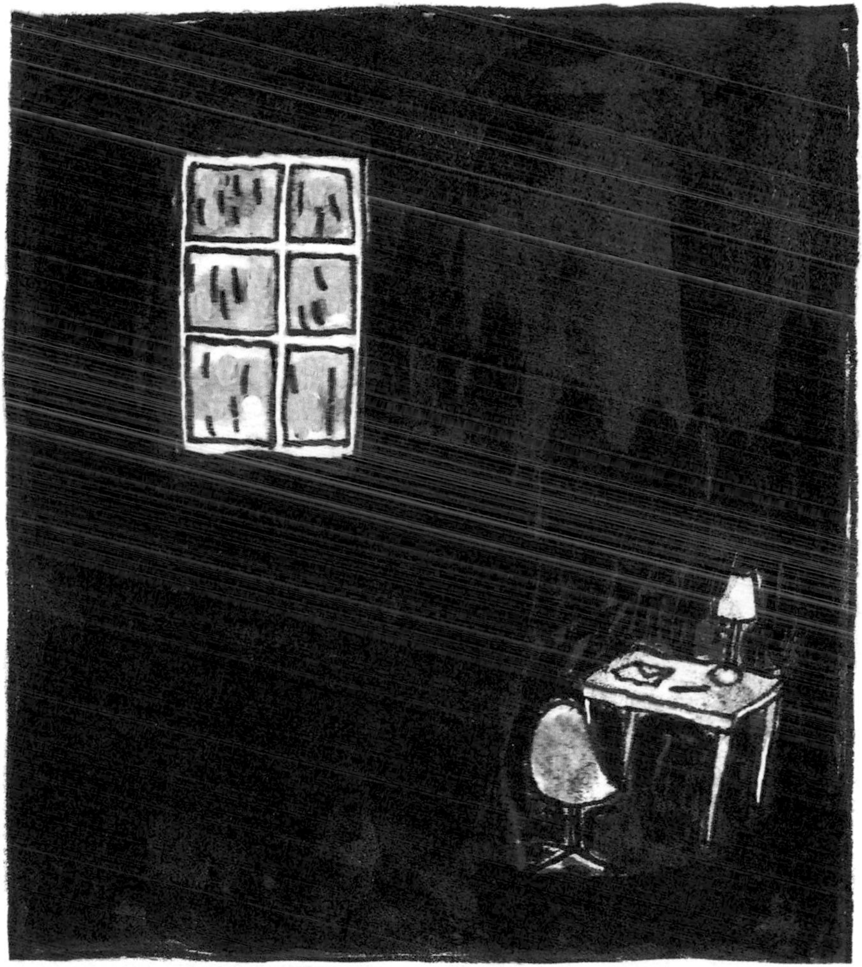

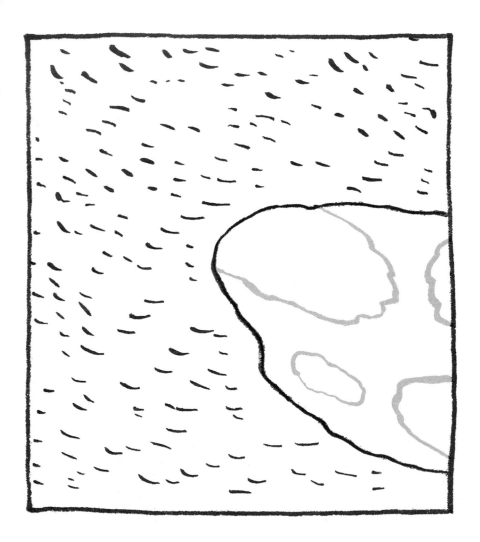

MAYBE YOU
DON'T FEEL
THE SAME
FRIEND-LOVE

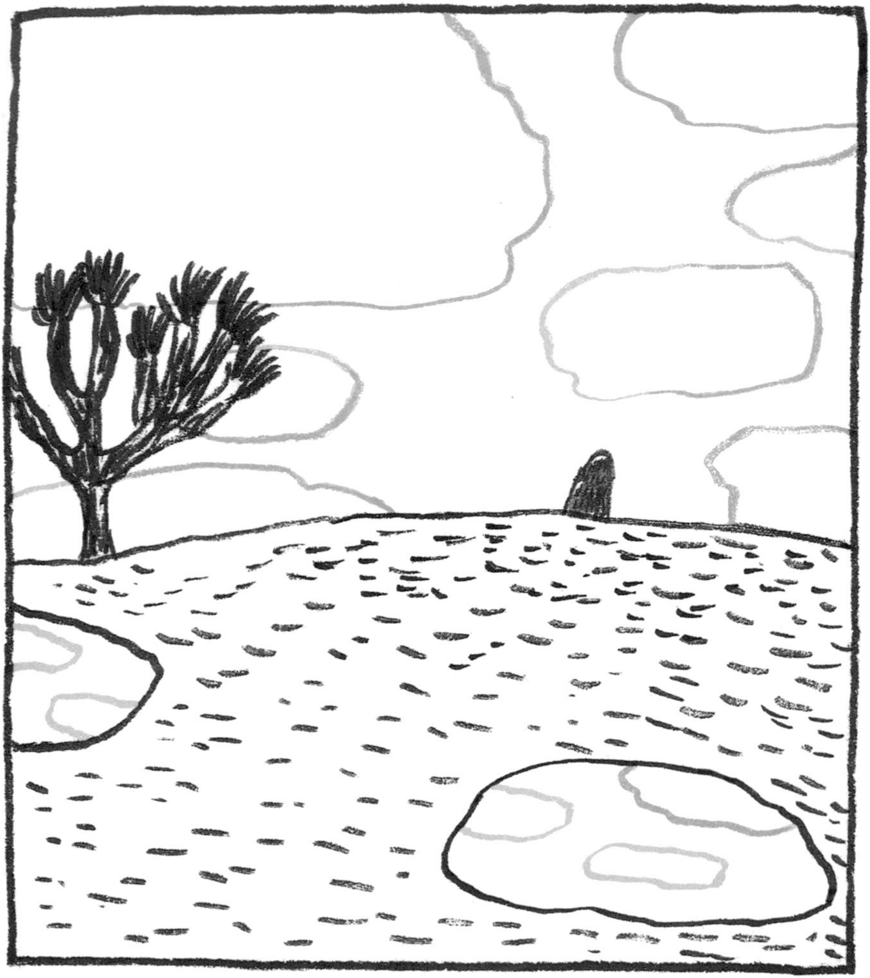

THAT I FEEL
FOR YOU.

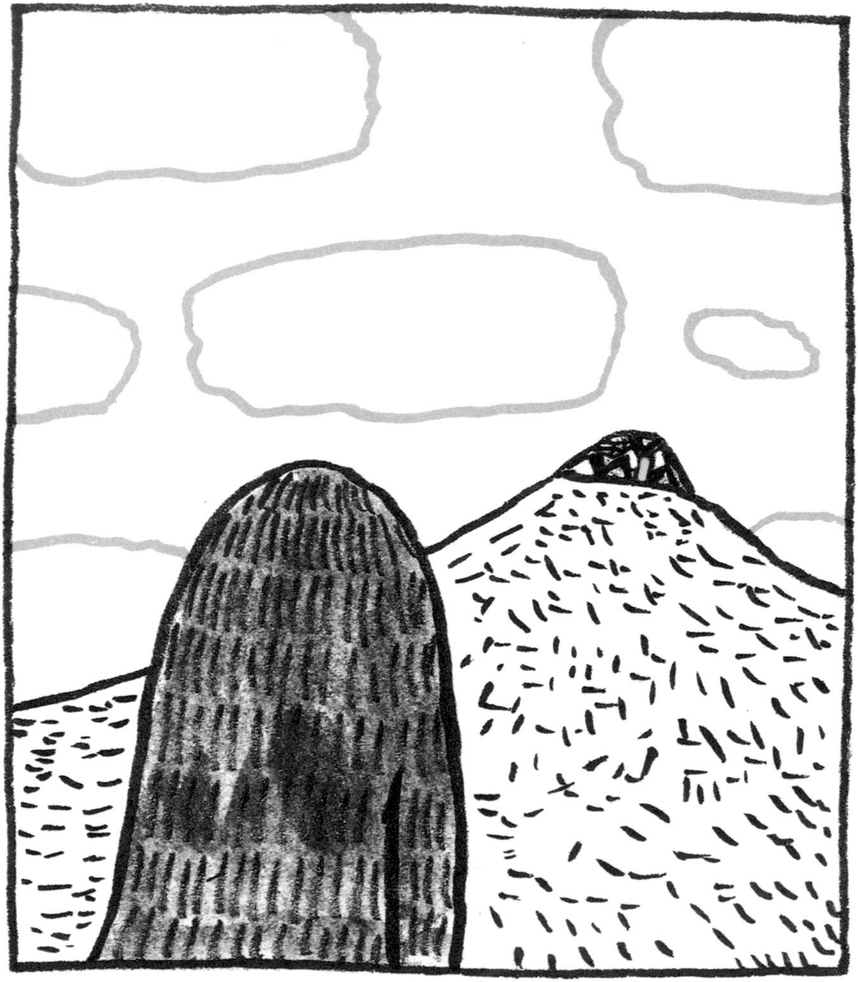

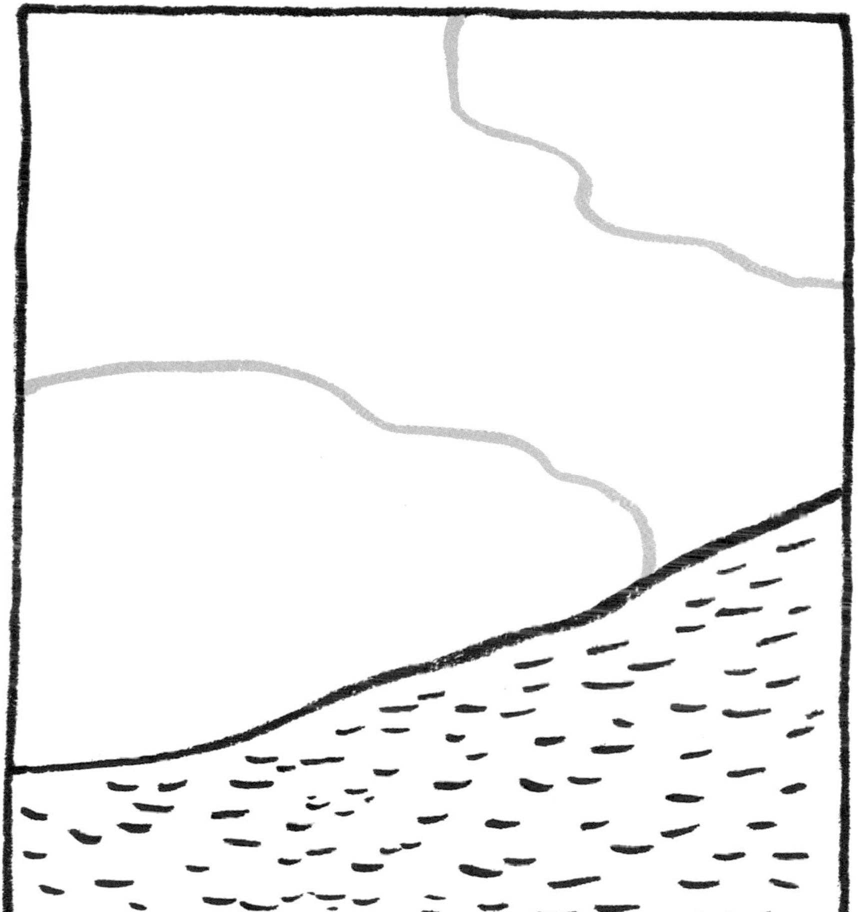

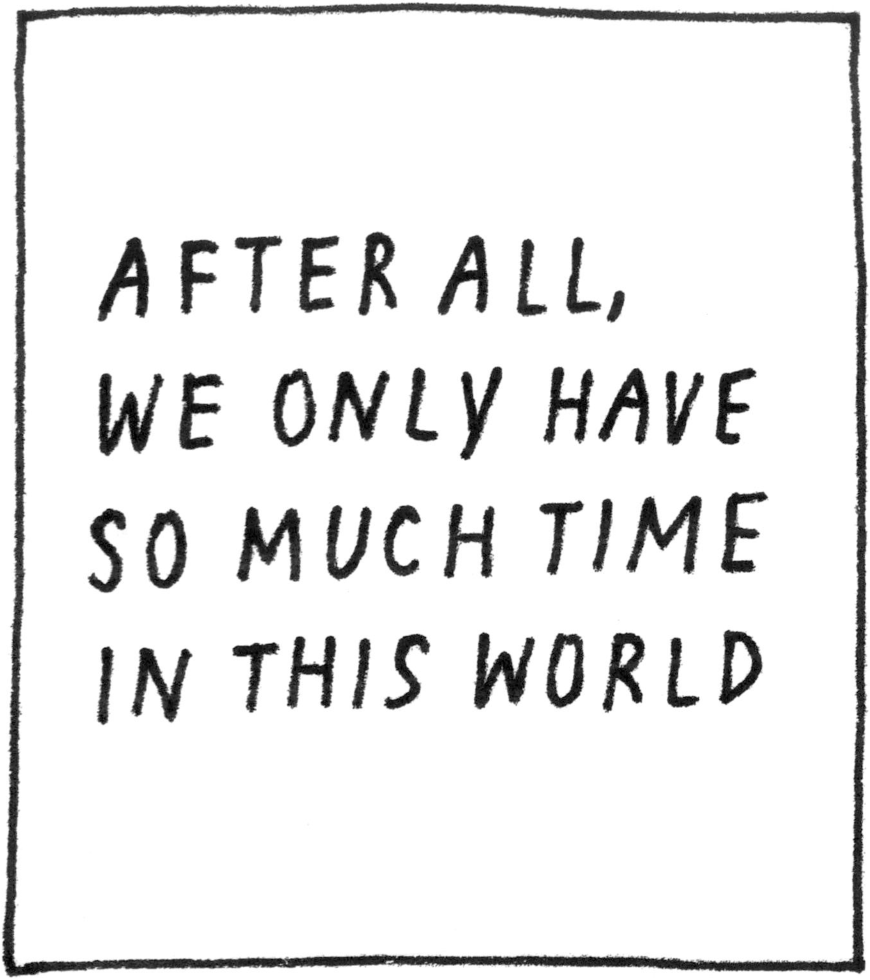
AFTER ALL, WE ONLY HAVE SO MUCH TIME IN THIS WORLD

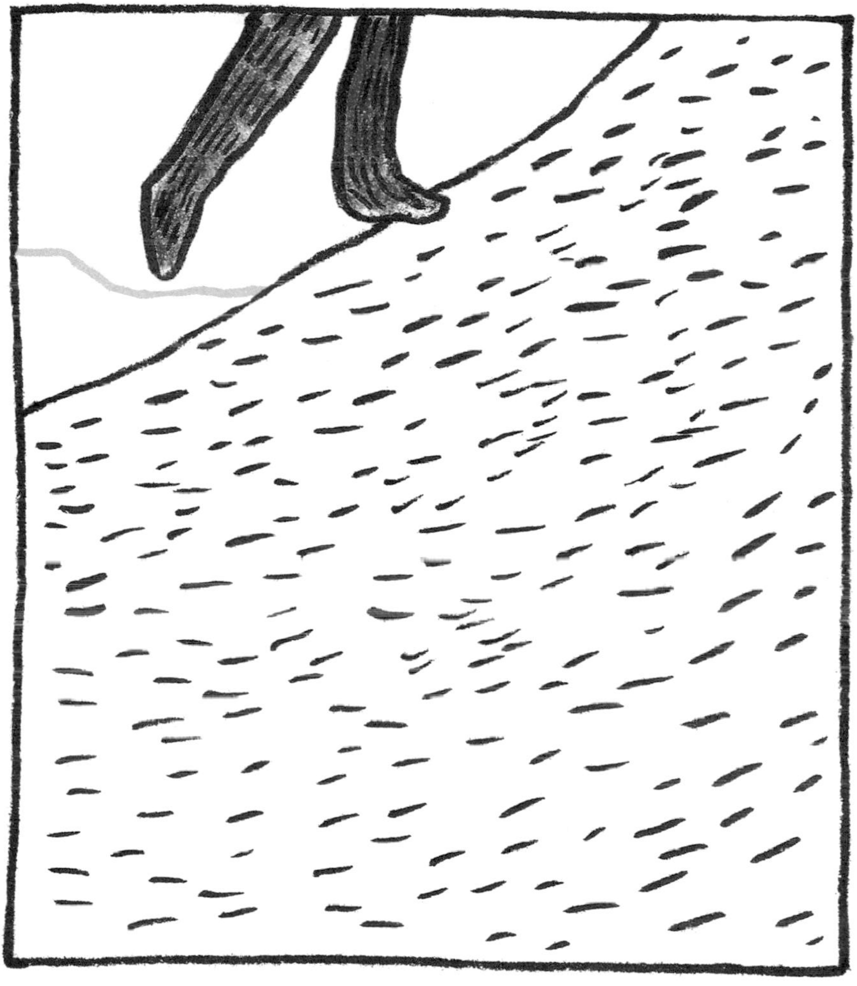

TO ONLY HAVE
SO MANY
FRIENDS.

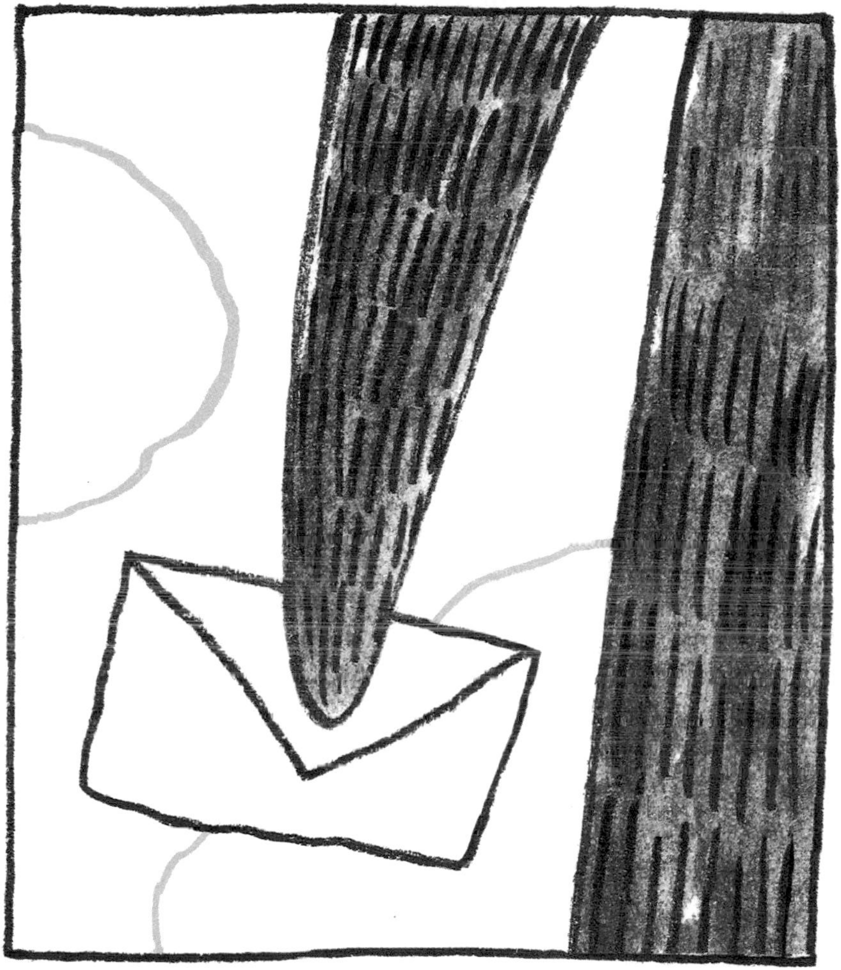

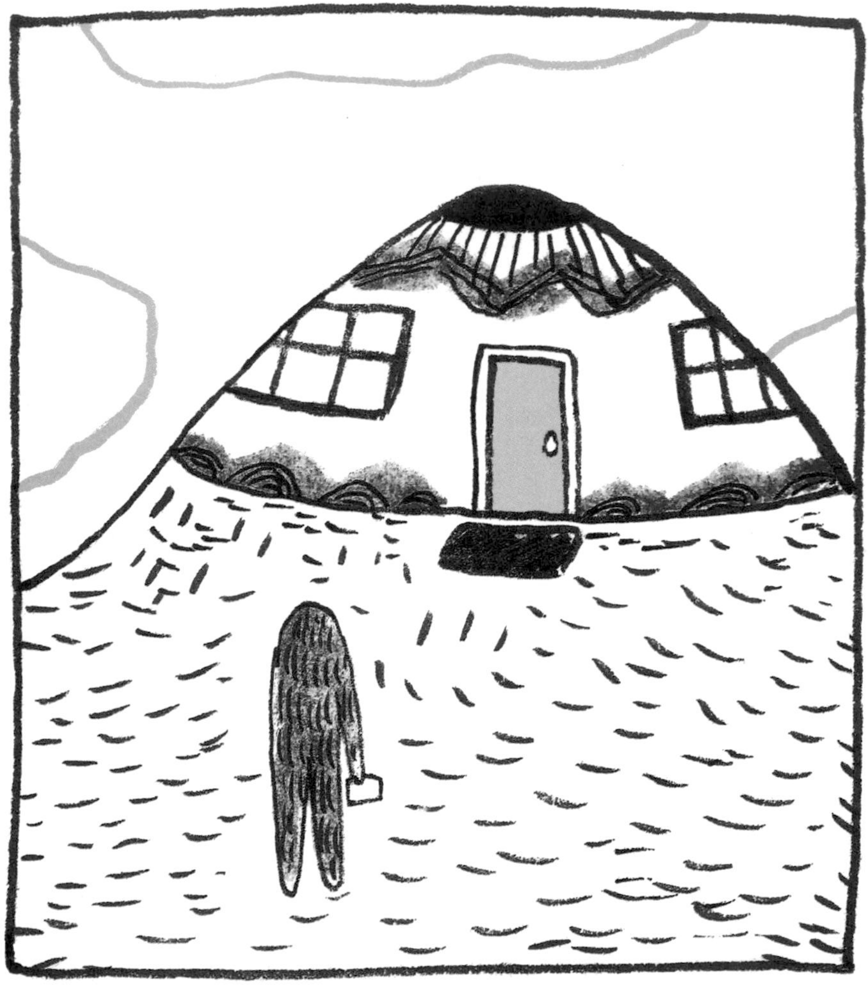

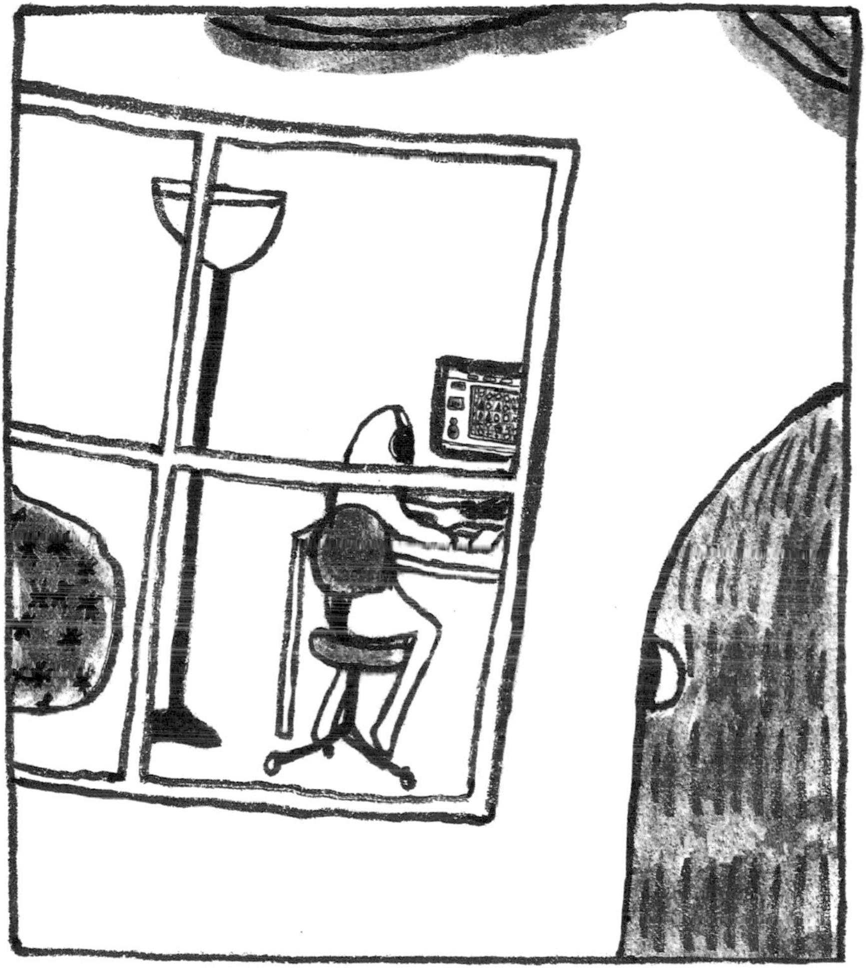

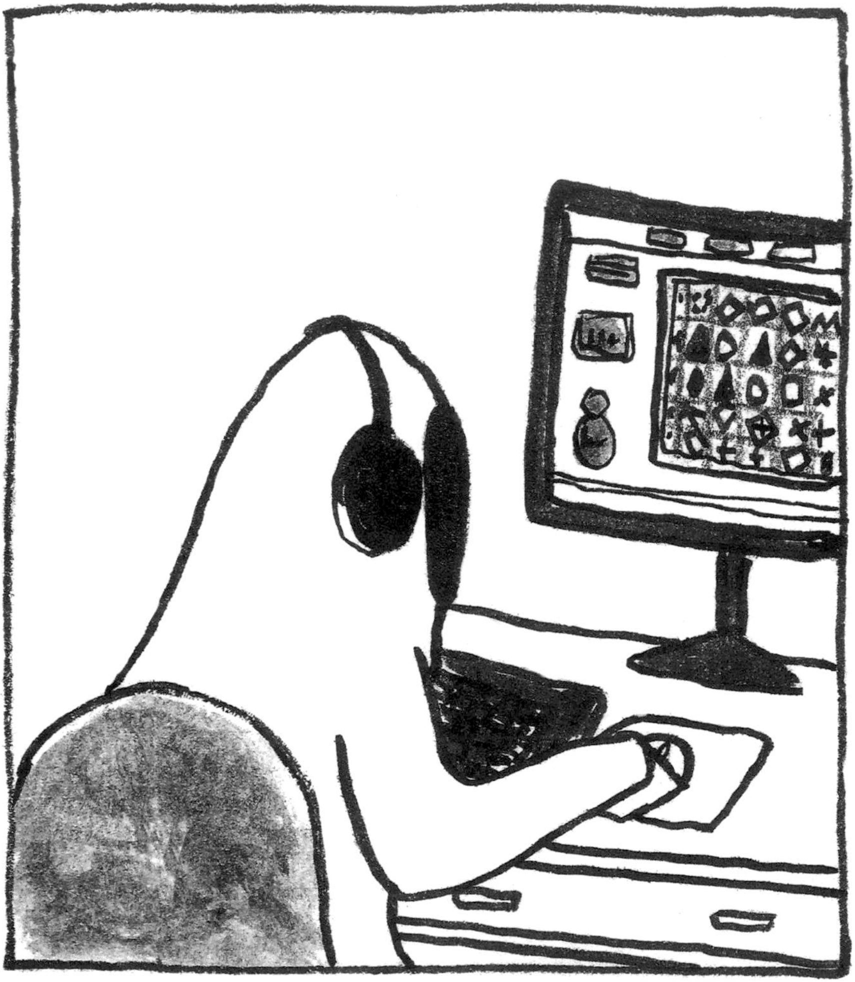

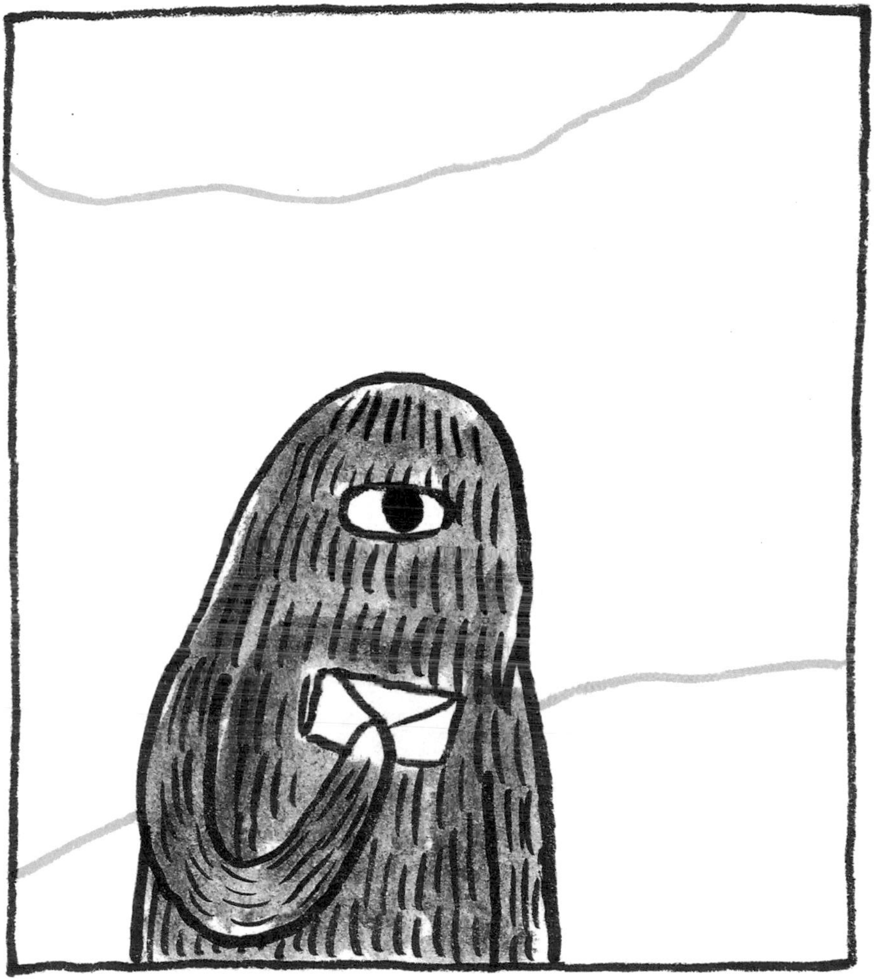

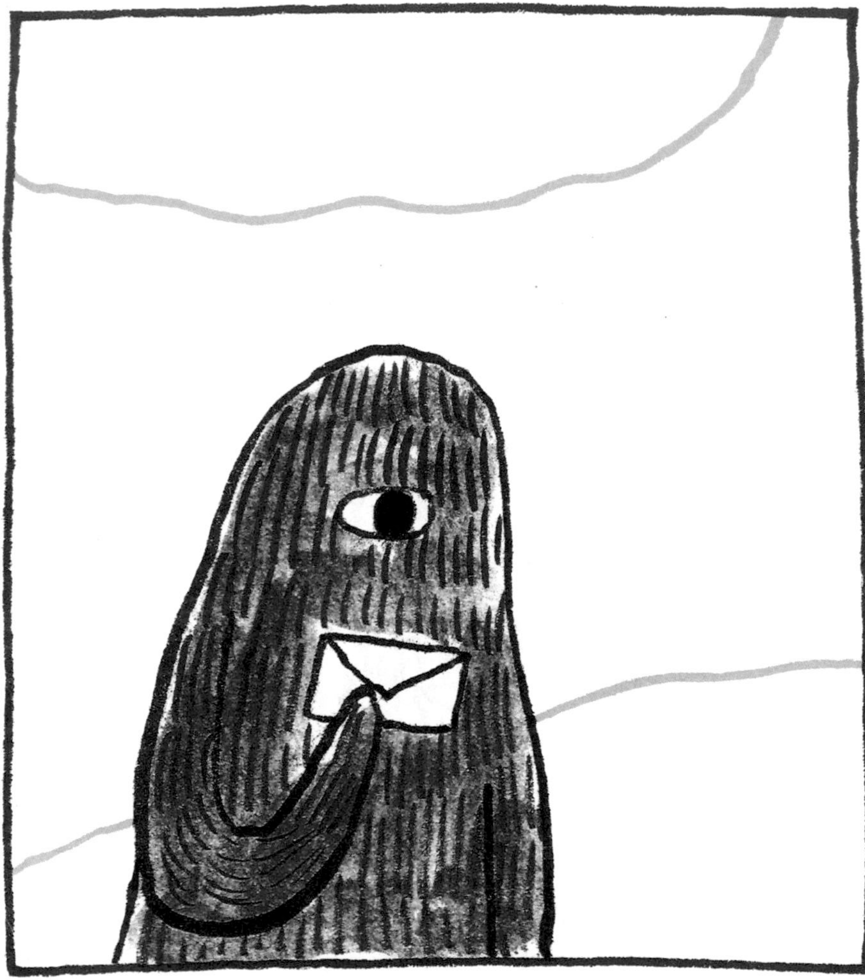

WELL,
ANYWAY.

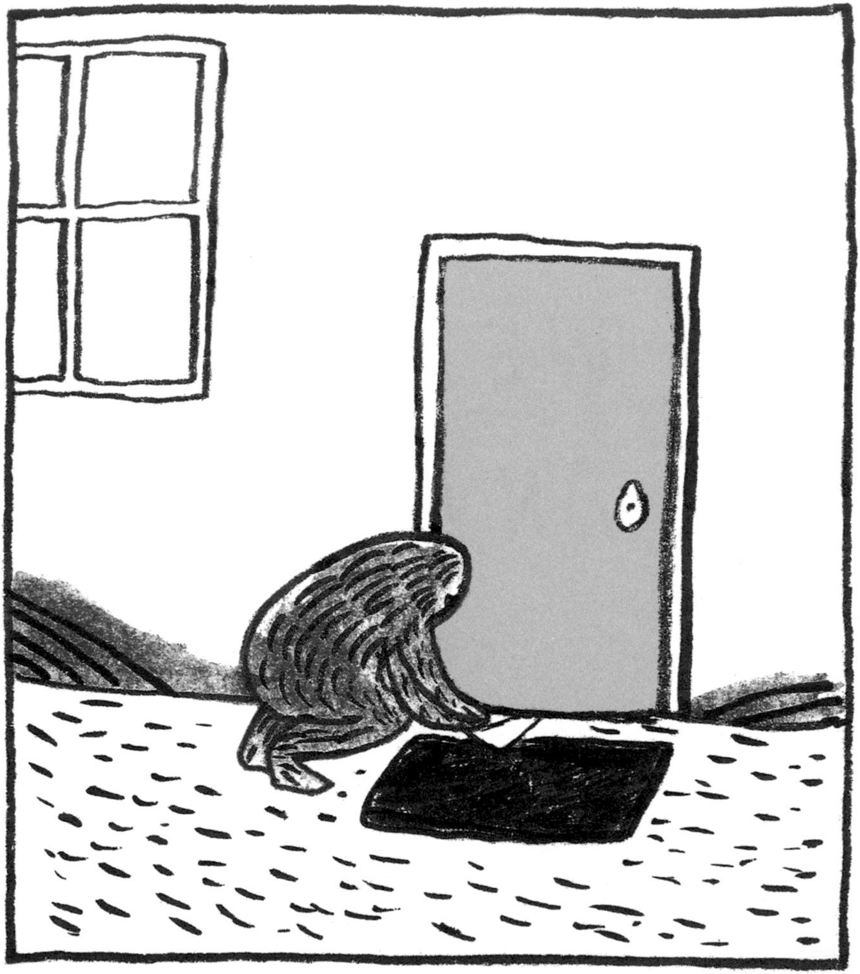

THANKS FOR
READING THIS.

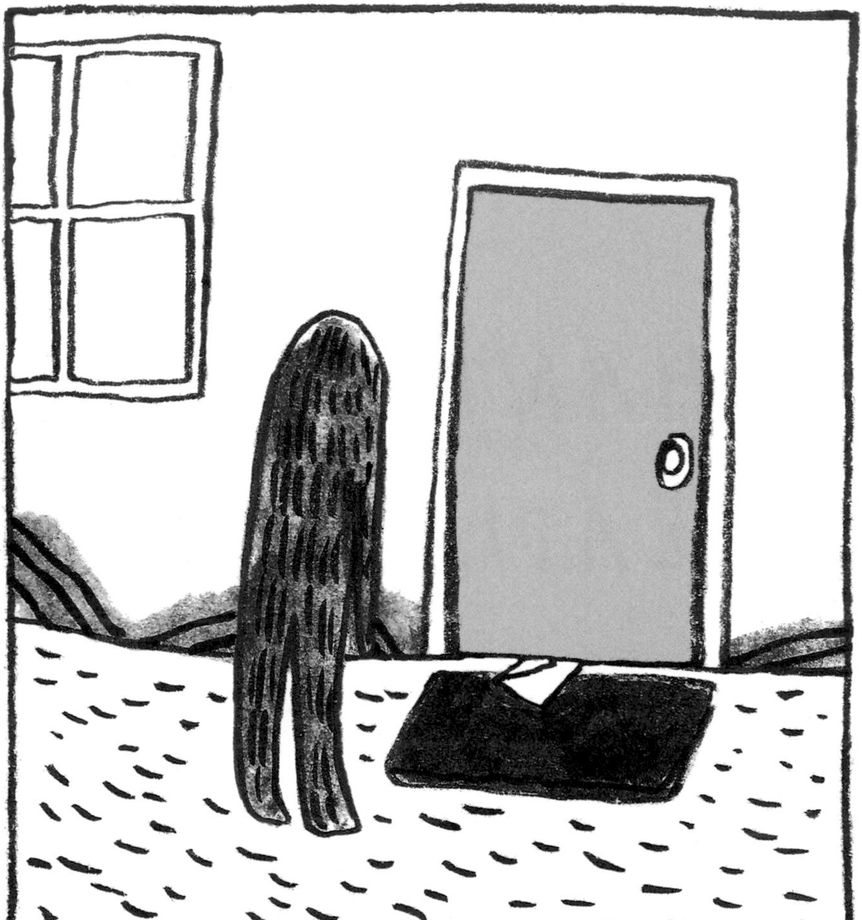

I HOPE YOU ARE DOING WELL.

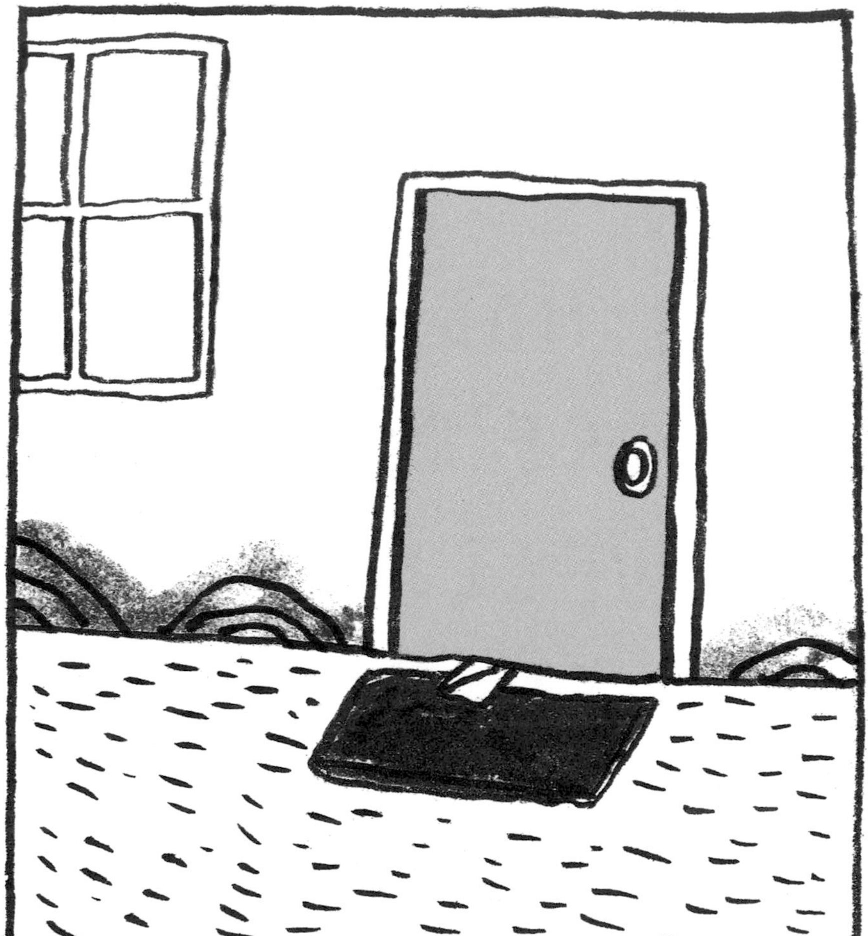

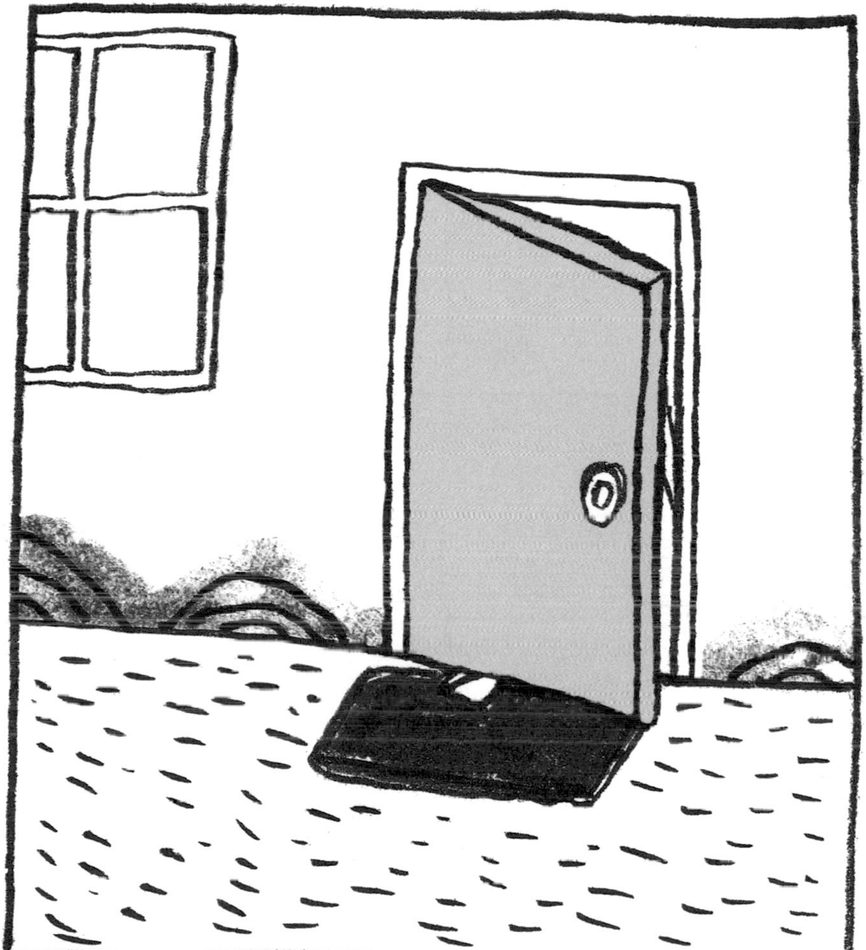

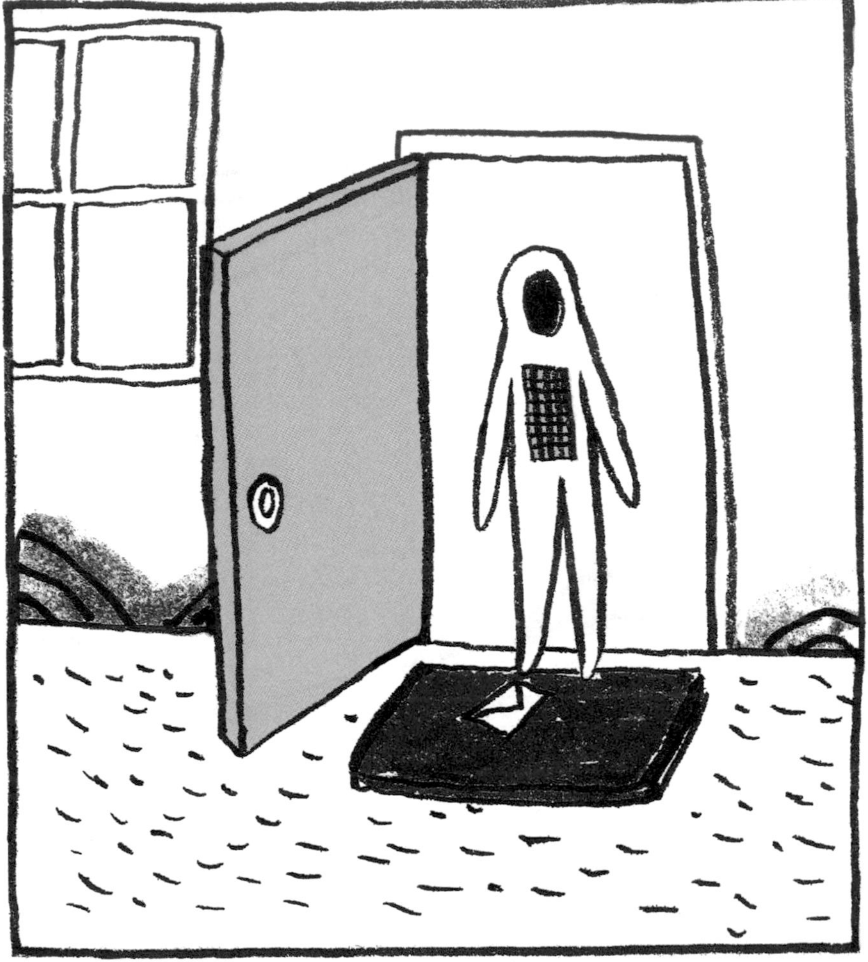

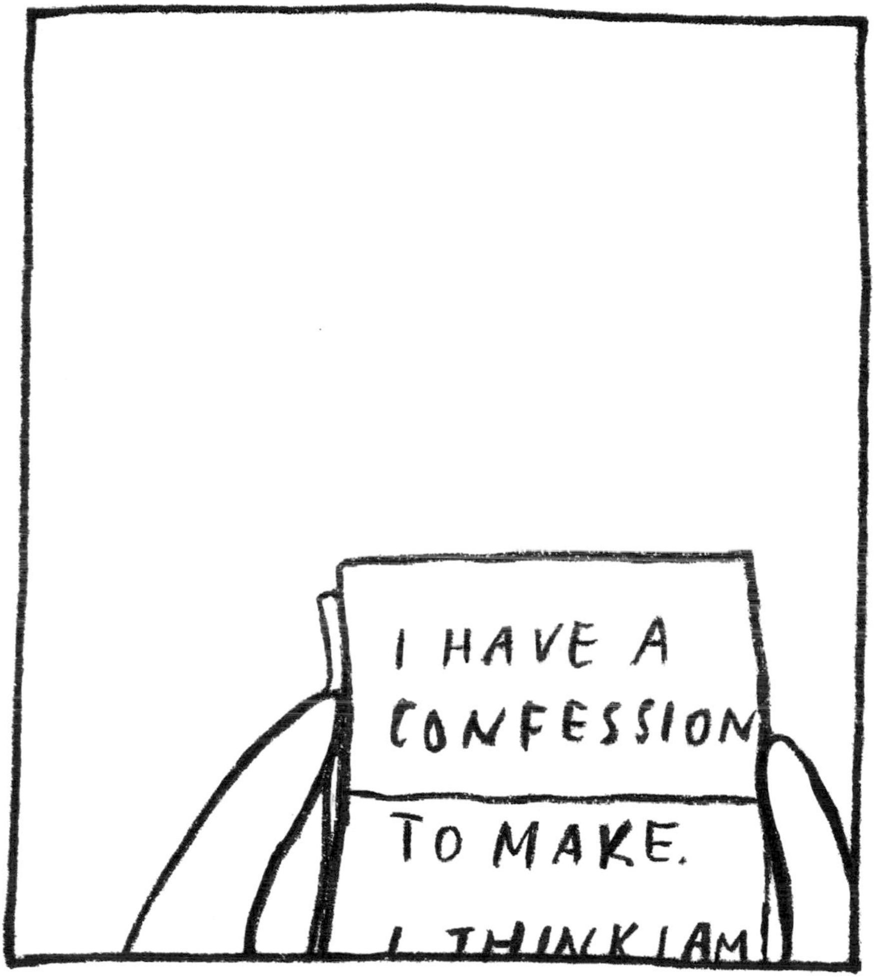
I HAVE A CONFESSION
TO MAKE.
I THINK I AM

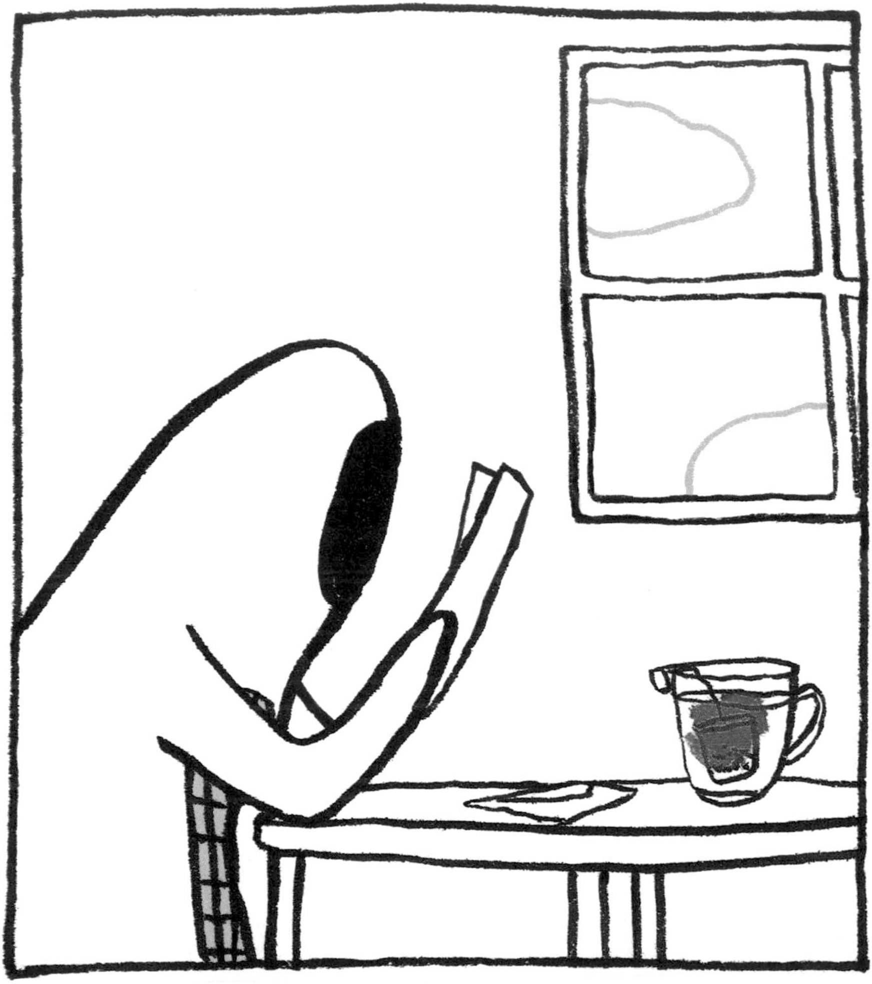

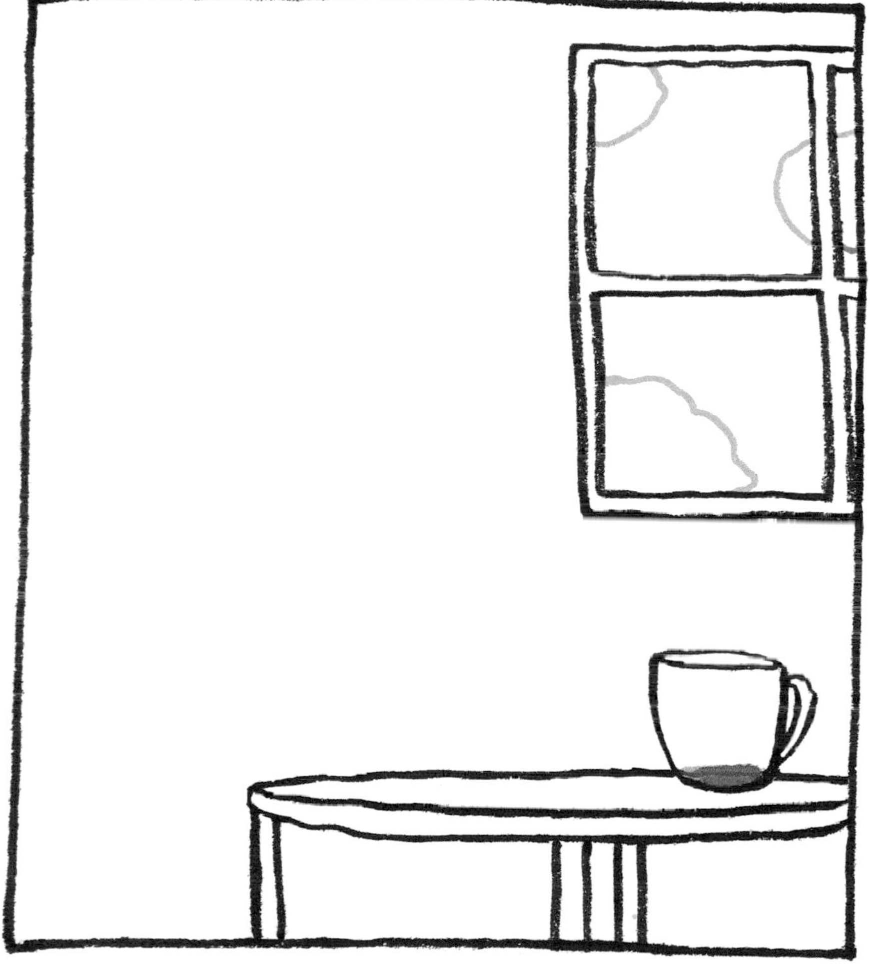

Acknowledgments

Thank you to everyone who made this book possible.

To all the countless readers from all over the world who read and shared *FRIEND-LOVE* when it was first posted online. Jesse Sposato for giving *FRIEND-LOVE* its original online home at *Sadie Magazine*. My agent Laurie Abkemeier for all of her valuable guidance in my first venture as a published author. My wonderful editor Brendan O'Neill and the rest of the Adams Media team for all of their amazing work.

To all of my not-so-secret friend-loves.

To Uncle Reg for being the best fan ever.

To my Mom and Dad for always supporting my artistic dreams from childhood to adulthood.

To my partner David for being the best friend-love and love-love that I could possibly ask for.

Lastly, I cannot forget the friend-loves of my past who have been the original inspiration for creating this book in the first place.
Wherever you all are, I hope you are doing well.

About the Author

Yumi Sakugawa is a comic book artist and illustrator based in Southern California. A graduate of the fine art program of University of California, Los Angeles, Yumi is a regular comic contributor for The Rumpus and Wonderhowto. com. Her illustrations and comics have been featured on Buzzfeed, Lifehacker, *PAPERMAG*, Apartment Therapy, and all over Tumblr. Her short comic story "Mundane Fortunes for the Next Ten Billion Years" was selected as a Notable Comic of 2012 by the Best American Comics anthology editors. Visit her on the web at *www.yumisakugawa.com.*